# The Priory and Medieval Hospitals of Nantwich and Wybunbury

*including: the Royal Benefactors of Nantwich Church; the Knights Hospitaller; and the Guild of the Holy Cross*

Charles E. S. Fairey

2023

*Front Cover:*
*Image based upon the North-Western Perpendicular Window of the Chancel of St Mary's Church, Nantwich with a Crusader Cross and Monk Figurine*

*Rear Cover:*
*The Geometry of St Mary's Church Tower and Vaulted Ceiling with a modern Pilgrim Token*

© **Charles E. S. Fairey 2023**


Charles E. S. Fairey's Historian Website @
https://sites.google.com/site/charlesfaireyhistorian/


*First Published 2023*


The rights of the author to this work has
been asserted by him in accordance with the Copyright,
Design and Patents Act, 1993.


All rights reserved. No part of this publication may be
reproduced, stored in a retrieval system or transmitted in any
form or by any means, electronic, mechanical, photocopying,
recording or otherwise without the prior permission of the
author: Charles E. S. Fairey.


For the avoidance of doubt, this includes reproduction of any
image in this book on an internet site.

# Contents

|  | Page |
|---|---|
| Foreword | 5 |
| Introduction | 7 |
| The Hospital and Chapel of St Nicholas (Hospital Street, Nantwich) | 11 |
| The Knights Hospitaller and Nantwich | 37 |
| Sir Nicholas Colfox, Knight and Chaplain Friend of King Richard II Prior of the Hospital of St Nicholas | 51 |
| The Royal Benefactors of Nantwich St Mary's "Hidden in Plain Sight" | 55 |
| Sir David Cradock, Knight Friend of King Richard II Founder of Nantwich (St Mary's) Church? | 87 |
| The Priory & The Hospital and Chapel of St Lawrence (Welsh Row, Nantwich) | 93 |
| The Hospital of the Holy Cross and St George (Wybunbury) | 143 |
| Medieval Hospitals | 149 |
| The Guild of the Holy Cross and Nantwich | 157 |
| Endnotes & References | 177 |
| Acknowledgements | 187 |
| Bibliography | 188 |

**St Nicholas, St George, and St Lawrence,
Stained Glass Windows,
Chester Cathedral Cloisters**

*"Now My Eyes Are Open
I Can See I Can See
What Was Long
Hidden From Me"*

# Foreword

It is painful to try to imagine the amount of documentary evidence of the history of Nantwich which has been lost down the centuries. By contrast, it is a delight to benefit from the diligence of local historians who have sought to research, preserve and interpret what little is available. The range of publications and the thriving museum are healthy signs of a town aware that an understanding of its roots is essential to its continued flourishing.

It is a work that continues, and while James Hall's history may be the "Bible" as far as Nantwich is concerned, it is not exhaustive, nor the last word on what it covers. Modestly titled "A History of the Town and Parish of Nantwich", it implies the possibility of others, and maybe invites them.

It is therefore a joy to see such labour of love continue, and a privilege for me to write a foreword to this latest contribution to the genre, a bold and painstakingly detailed history by Charles Fairey. This work could have been distilled to a brief summary of the more eye-catching claims, but Charles has done a service to future generations by showing his working and declaring his sources. The result is a work that no-one seriously interested in the history of the town can ignore.

A modern reader may find the combination of hospital and church history to be incongruous, but of course the division of the health of body and soul would be equally puzzling to the medieval mind. We think it is modern to be holistic, but the trend in that direction is, like much that we call progress, a recovery of lost wisdom.

Naturally, I am especially interested in this book's theories about the origin of St Mary's Church, not least the possibility of more royal connection and depiction than we have thought. There is no better time than a Coronation year to be advancing such ideas and encouraging people to recognise royal figures and crowns around the building, as we will do with a children's trail this year.

This book makes a significant contribution to the important task of reading the church. It is true that there is a degree of playfulness in certain aspects of the decoration of St Mary's, but nothing is random; there is a high level of order and meaning. By comparison with similar styles in other churches, much can be understood in general terms, but specific local interpretation, as found here, is hard work, and to be commended.

This book makes an impressive effort to answer some important historical questions. Charles has moved the conversation forward, and offered exciting new ways to understand our church and town. He has done a service to Nantwich and I hope his work stimulates close attention to our heritage and fresh discussion of our past.

Mark Hart

*Rector of St Mary's Church, Nantwich*
*St David's Day, 1st March 2023*

# Introduction

The South Cheshire town of Nantwich, known for its historic buildings (and in the past, the second largest county settlement after Chester), had a number of medieval hospitals, as well as a religious establishment referred to as 'Namptwich Priory'. This priory was thought to be a monastic cell relating to the nearby Cistercian monastery known as Combermere Abbey.

Most townsfolk will know that 'Hospital Street' takes its name from a medieval hospital dedicated to St Nicholas once standing at its eastern end.

Most will also know that at the western end of Welsh Row, another medieval hospital dedicated to St Lawrence also stood, whose actual site was still debated.

As well as Nantwich's two medieval hospitals, and the possible priory (which is also thought to have existed near to St Lawrence's) there was also another medieval hospital at the nearby village of Wybunbury, dedicated to the Holy Cross and St George.

On the following pages, we discuss the history of each establishment, and their historic associations, as well as reveal the actual location of St Lawrence's Hospital and Chapel, as well as the supposed site of the Priory.

We also try to verify what 'Namptwich Priory' was, and discuss the little information that exists about it.

We also briefly discuss the Almshouses (which were built near to both medieval hospitals and the priory), and were also sometimes known as 'hospitals'.

We also reveal historic links to the Crusaders and their military religious orders, especially the Knights Hospitaller, and their links with the town, its Church, and St Nicholas' Hospital and Chapel.

We also discuss the people linked with the history of the hospitals, and two people specifically relating to them, the Hospitallers, or the Church.

We also uncover the 'Guild of the Holy Cross' who were linked with St Mary's Church in Nantwich, and the town's Guildhall. They were also likely linked with the medieval hospital at Wybunbury.

We also reveal some important historic detail relating to the fantastic history of St Mary's Church, which has laid 'hidden in plain sight' all this time, and that its main benefactors were ultimately royal.

*Charles E. S. Fairey, January 2023*

*(Local Historian, Nantwich Museum Research Group Volunteer, and Malbank School & Sixth Form Student (Sept 1990- June 1997))*

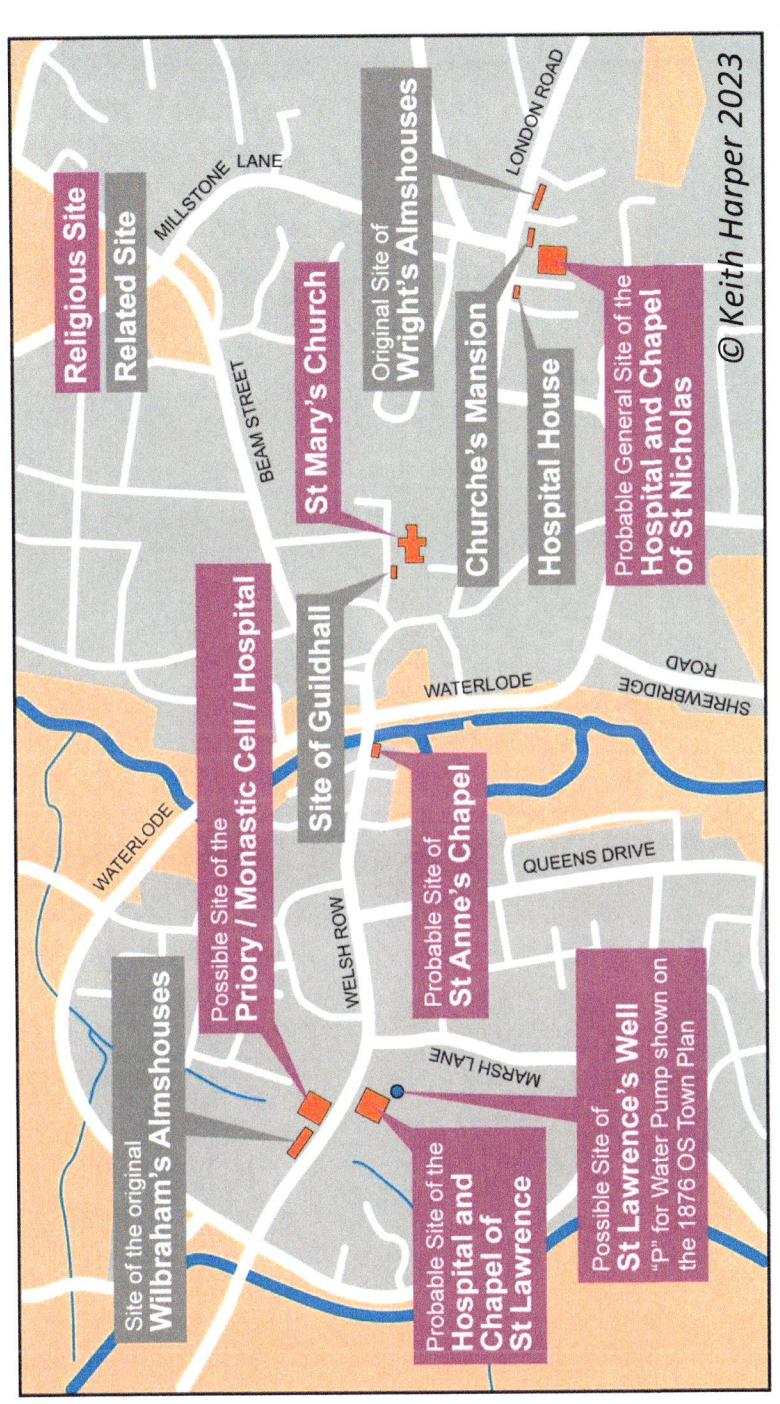

Location of the Religious and Related Sites in Nantwich discussed in this book

Created by Keith Harper (Nantwich Museum) (Reproduced with his permission)

**Location of the Religious Sites around Nantwich discussed in this book**

Created by Keith Harper (Nantwich Museum) (Reproduced with his permission)

© Keith Harper 2023

# The Hospital and Chapel of St Nicholas
# (Hospital Street, Nantwich)

Nantwich's first medieval hospital was called 'The Hospital and Chapel of St Nicholas' and is thought to have been founded by the first baron of Nantwich, William Malbank, in 1083-84. The hospital gave its name to the road which ran from its location on the eastern outskirts of the town, to the town centre; i.e. Hospital Street.

If the Hospital was in fact founded in 1083-84, it would make it one of the earliest hospital foundations in medieval England. Other sources suggest a circa 1087 date, but this too is early, and therefore important too.

Another medieval hospital with an early foundation, but for the treatment of lepers, was founded in c1084 on the Canterbury to London road at Harbledown, Kent. This too was dedicated to St Nicholas, and was founded by Lanfranc, Archbishop of Canterbury 1070-89, to house 60 lepers.

St Nicholas' Hospital wasn't controlled by a religious house (i.e. a monastery or abbey, or the Church, etc), and its associated chapel, was often referred to as a 'Free Chapel'. This means that it was either separately controlled, or that it was part of a secular order which wasn't under Church or Monastic control (see later). This meant that it was in the care of a secular clerk, i.e. a chaplain.

The chaplain might also be the Prior, Master, or Warden of the hospital, charged with the duties of running the institution, officiating over the pilgrims, poor and ill people, housed within, both in a spiritual and caring manner, along with a number of laymen he would have presided over. Often the chaplains or masters would have held other offices in the locality or elsewhere, but whilst not present at the hospital, they would have left it in the charge of brethren, sisters, novices, and lay folk.

After the barons Malbank, namely: William, the first baron of Nantwich; his son Hugh, the second baron of Nantwich; and his grandson, William, the third baron of Nantwich; due to the third baron only having three daughters as heirs, the barony of Nantwich was divided between them. This meant that the advowson (the right to appoint a clerk in holy orders to the benefice) of St Nicholas' Chapel and Hospital, passed through the Bassett and Burnell families, and later to the Lovell family, and then to a member of the Stanley family, (see later), before this religious establishment finally ended its long life at the Dissolution of the Monasteries, in the mid 16$^{th}$ century.

According to **'The History of Cheshire, Volume 3, George Ormerod, 1882, Page 449'**, William Malbank, baron of Wich Malbank [Nantwich], [in 1083-84], *"granted to the Hospital certain lands and tenements, which occur in an enrolled writ of livery to Master Alan de Newerk, clerk [in holy orders], Rector of the Hospital, as having been taken into the Prince's hands on an Inq[uisition] [dating to 1403-04] 5$^{th}$ [year of the reign of] Henry IV. (Recog[nisance] Rolls 8 [1406-07] & 9 [1407-08] H[enry] IV. M. 8d.)"*, and that *"it occurs in the Lichfield Registers, under the several designations of the chantry, the free chapel, and the hospital of St. Nicholas"*.

St Nicholas' Chapel and Hospital was a place for pilgrims, i.e. it gave pilgrims hospitality, i.e. food, drink and shelter, whilst travelling, as well as being a house for the poor, ill of health, injured, elderly, and destitute. Much the same as abbeys, priories, and hospitals, did across the country, and where the original form of the word 'hotel' derives from, a hostel, or hospice, i.e. a hospital, and hospitality. The hospital also gave alms (the charitable giving of money or food) to the poor of Nantwich derived from its income from hospitality, tithes, tolls, charitable gifts, and rents on the property it held, as well as its salthouses.

Combermere Abbey also operated as a place for travellers and pilgrims to stay, although chiefly, it operated as a monastery for its abbot, brethren, and lay workers. It was recorded in historic records, that the gentry/knights and their entourage, sometimes took advantage of this hospitality, when essentially it was meant for the poor, pilgrims, and, those of lesser means, travelling the country, and those requiring care, to be housed.

***The Pilgrim Bench End to the Dean's (once the Abbot's) Stall,
to the right of the west entrance to Chester Cathedral's Quire***

The supposed site of St Nicholas' Hospital at the eastern end of the town, and at the eastern end of the street which acquired its name from the Hospital, i.e. Hospital Street, is on the main road through the town of Nantwich. It was also a major routeway between London and the City of Chester, and on an important pilgrimage route to St Werburgh's Shrine and Abbey, in Chester, which is now known as Chester Cathedral, as well as St John's Church, by the Amphitheatre. Thus the religious establishment was perfectly situated for the travelling pilgrims, at the entrance or exit of the town. The earliest mention of the name of the road that ran past St Nicholas' as 'Hospital Street', or similar, in historic deeds, is in c1300.[1]

It would have proved a worthy spiritual investment, to establish the religious house or hospital for pilgrims, and for the poor and infirm, because Mass would have been said for its founder, in its dedicated chapel, for the immortality of his soul, and its spiritual passage to heaven.

If this hospital had in fact been granted by its founder to a religious order as its benefactor(s), the hospital would have raised money for them and its day-to-day running (and for its Master and Chaplain to carry out his duties), by way of care and more lucratively, providing food, drink and shelter. Likewise, those paying or being charitable for their received hospitality; would also be raising money for the care of those also housed in the hospital, due to ill health, age, or due to their poor circumstances.

The abuse of Combermere Abbey's hospitality is revealed in **'Cheshire Under the Three Edwards. A History of Cheshire, Volume 5, H. J. Hewitt, 1967, Page 92'**, where we are told that the abbey was one of four monastic houses to complain to Edward, the Black Prince in 1351, about the costs it was accruing due to providing hospitality to guests and their servants, horses and hunting hounds.

Other religious houses who complained were St Werburgh's Abbey, Chester, and Vale Royal Abbey, Winsford, who had also been overburdened by local people seeking hospitality.[2]

And in **'Wrenbury and Marbury, Local History Group, F. A. Latham (editor), 1999, Page 24'**, it is speculated that because of the abbey's proximity to the road from Chester to Shrewsbury, meant that the cost of its hospitality to travellers was a drain on its resources.

< *Saint Nicholas in Stained Glass, South Aisle Window, by Harry Clarke 1919, St Mary's Church, Nantwich*

George Ormerod in his *'The History of Cheshire, Volume 3, 1882, Pages 449-450'*, gives us *"the following admissions of [St Nicholas's Hospital's] Masters [Rectors] or Wardens [which] are taken from ... the [transcripts of the original] Lichfield Episcopal Registers"* (translated from Medieval Latin into its English equivalent, where able) as follows:-

| Admission | Hospital Master | Patron | Vacated by |
|---|---|---|---|
| 1330, to, and before? | Master Robert de Marchomlegh | | |
| 1330, 4$^{th}$ December | Alexander le Blount, Priest | Lord John de Hanlowe, Knight | After the death of Master Robert de Marchomle, the last Rector |
| 1350, to, and before? | Master Thomas Corbet | | |
| 1350, 15$^{th}$ May | Roger de Alleton, Priest | Edward, registered first son in the County of Chester, recorded custodian, son and heir of Lord John Lovel, Knight | After the death of Master Thomas Corbet, the last Chaplain (of the chantry or chapel, of St Nicholas of Wychmauban [Wich Malbank [Nantwich]]) |
| 1354, 12$^{th}$ August | John de Newenham, Chaplain | Edward son, custodian and in the custody of John Lovell, to minor | After the resignation of Roger de Allerton, the last Chaplain |
| 1364, 12$^{th}$ March | Nicholas Rivell, Priest | Bishop appointed | (After the Hospital and Chapel of St Nicholas de Namptwych [Nantwich] became vacant) |
| 1365, 3$^{rd}$ October | Roger son of William de Blakhurst | Edmund Everard, Knight, Attorney General, on behalf of John Lovell de Tichemerssh | (After the Free Chapel of St Nicholas de Wyco Malbano [Nantwich] became vacant) |
| 1374, 20$^{th}$ day of April | John de Ormeshened, Priest | Lord John Lovell, Knight and Lord de Tichemersch. | After the resignation of Master Roger de Blakehurste, 19 April |
| 1376, 8$^{th}$ day of December | Master John de Wodehous, Priest | Lord John Lovell, Knight | After the resignation of John de Ormeshened, last custodian, 27$^{th}$ day of November last |

| | | | |
|---|---|---|---|
| 1395, the last day of October | Thomas Hyne, Priest | To us men of God John Lord Lovell and de Holand | After the death of Master John Wodehous, Dean of Chester, last recorded ecclesiastical income, August last |
| 1396, 27th day of March | Master Alan de Newwerk, Priest | To us men of God John Lord de Lovell and de Holand | After the resignation of Master Thomas Hyne, last custodian or Master |
| 1425 | Ranulph le Bruyn, Priest | Reverend previously Lord William, by the Grace of God, ? and ? ? ? ? | |
| 1460 to, and before? | Master Thomas Heywode | | |
| 1460, 15th day of November | Master Thomas Friston, Chaplain | | After the death of Master Thomas Heywode, last Master or custodian |
| 1468, 21st day of October | Ranulph Egerton, Priest | The Honourable Lord Richard, companion of Warewici [Warwick] and ? Lord of Bergevenny here changed ? ? Lord de Lovell | After the resignation of Master Thomas ffryston, last Master or custodian of the Hospital or Chapel |
| 1477, 28th day of May | Richard Egerton, Priest | Illustrious without equal? Prince Edward, First son of the King, etc, ? | After the resignation of Ranulph Egerton, last Master and custodian |
| 1506, 4th day of February | Thomas Blythe, Priest | Feared without equal? Lord now King (In old Chester Register, Henry King of England) | After the resignation of Master Richard Egerton, the last custodian |
| 1531, 11 day of December | Mr William Gwyn, Priest | Excellent without equal? to the ? Principal and Lord now Lord Henry VIII | After the death of Master Thomas Blythe, the last incumbent |
| 1541, 9th day of April | Master William Hill, Bachelor of Canon Law | Excellent and Powerful without equal? at ? Principal and Lord Henry VIII | After the natural death of Master William Gvoyn, last Master or custodian |
| **DISSOLVED:** | **1548** | | |

Ormerod goes on to include that the two last Masters of the Chapel and Hospital of St Nicholas, were: William Gwynne, in the general Ecclesiastical Survey of 1534-35; and William Hill, late incumbent of the Chapel of St Nicholas, until 1556, when he was living on a pension of 100 shillings a year.

As well as the list of Masters of the Hospital and Chapel of St Nicholas, above; we find that according to *'A History of the County of Chester: Volume 3, Victoria County History, 1980, Pages 186-187'*, the following Chaplains, Masters, Wardens or Rectors, are as follows:-

| Hospital Master | Years | Source |
| --- | --- | --- |
| John | occurs 1259 | B.L. Harl. MS. 1967, f. 113v. He was chaplain of the hospital. Hall (*Nantwich*, 49) wrongly listed William de la Bach as warden in 131617: above, hospital of St. John. |
| Robert de Marchumleye | occurs 1323, died 1330 | *Cal. Pat.* 13214, 362; Lich. Jt. R.O., B/A/1/2, f. 106. |
| Alexander le Blount | presented 1330 | Lich. Jt. R.O., B/A/1/2, f. 106. |
| Thomas Corbet | died 1349 | Ibid. f. 127. He was chaplain of the chantry chapel of St. Nicholas. |
| Roger of Allerton | presented 1350, resigned 1353 | Ibid.; *Blk. Prince's Reg.* iii. 111. |
| John de Newenham | presented 1353 | *Blk. Prince's Reg.* iii. 111. He held prebends in Lich. cath.: Le Neve, *Fasti*, 1300-1541, *Cov. & Lich.* 21, 55, 66. |
| Nicholas Rivell | collated 1365 | *1st Reg. Stretton*, 166. |
| Roger de Blakhurst | presented 1365, resigned 1374 | Ibid. 166, 177. |
| John de Ormesheued | presented 1374, resigned 1377 | Ibid. 177, 180. |
| John Wodehouse | presented 1377, died 1395 | Ibid. 180; Lich. Jt. R.O., B/A/1/6, f. 60. He was dean of St. John's, Chester and chamberlain of Chester: *Ch. in Chester*, 1256. |
| Thomas Hyne | presented 1395, resigned 1396 | Lich. Jt. R.O., B/A/1/6, f. 60. |

| | | |
|---|---|---|
| Alan Newark, B.C.L. [Bachelor of Canon Law] | presented 1396, died 1412 | Ibid. f. 60v.; 36 *D.K.R.* 359; *Wills & Inventories*, i. 512. For details of his career see Emden, *Biog. Reg. Oxford*, ii. 13545. |
| Ralph le Bruyn | collated 1425 | *Reg. Chichele* (Cant. & York Soc.), i. 226. |
| Thomas Heywood | died 1460 | Lich. Jt. R.O., B/A/1/12, f. 98. |
| Thomas Friston | collated 1460, resigned 1468 | Ibid. ff. 98, 104. He had been chaplain of the hospital. |
| Ranulph Egerton | presented 1468, resigned 1477 | Ibid. ff. 104, 111. |
| Richard Egerton | presented 1477, resigned 1507 | Ibid. f. 111; B/A/1/14 i, f. 55. For his later offices and benefices see *V.C.H. Staffs*. iii. 287n. |
| Thomas Blythe | presented 1507, died 1531 | Lich. Jt. R.O., B/A/1/14 i, ff. 51, 68. He also held the prebend of Colwich in Lich. cath.: Le Neve, *Fasti, 13001541, Cov. & Lich.* 27. |
| William Gwyn | presented 1531, died 1540 | Lich. Jt. R.O., B/A/1/14 i, f. 48; B/A/1/14 iii, f. 38v. He also held the prebend of Stotfold in Lich. cath.: Le Neve, *Fasti, 13001541, Cov. & Lich.* 57. |
| William Hill, B.C.L. | presented 1541 | Lich. Jt. R.O., B/A/1/14 iii, f. 38v. He also held the prebend of Weeford in Lich. cath. and was 50 yrs. old in 1548: Le Neve, *Fasti, 13001541, Cov. & Lich.* 65; Hall, *Nantwich*, 51. See also Emden, *Biog. Reg. Oxford*, 150140, 310. |
| **DISSOLVED: 1548** | | |

James Hall in his **'A History of the Town and Parish of Nantwich or Wych-Malbank, Cheshire, 1883 (Republished 1972), Page 49'**, tells us that John ..., was the Chaplain of St Nicholas' Hospital in 1259, and that he appears as a witness to a historic deed of that date amongst the Wettenhall Charters (Harleian Manuscripts 1967 f. 113).

Eric Garton tells us in his **'Nantwich: Saxon to Puritan, 1972, Page 5'**, that John was the Chaplain of St Nicholas' Hospital in around 1280, and was the son of Henry Gogeli and Aldusa Lewis, the daughter of Richard Lewis. Henry, John's father, was a baker.

Eric Garton goes on to include that Thomas le Brol, was a carpenter of Nantwich, and that his daughter Avicia had married Richard Lewis, either Aldusa's father or brother. He also tells us that Thomas le Brol, or his ancestors, had acquired part of the lands of St Nicholas' Hospital, from the Knights Hospitaller, and that part of that land was inherited by Thomas' daughter Avicia. This and later transactions of the land, later with buildings upon it, through the families above, gives a good reason why John [Gogeli] became the chaplain of the Hospital and its Knights Hospitaller links (see next chapter).

This is evidenced, says Eric Garton, on **'Page 6'** of his history, by a historic deed that first defines the site and the buildings of the Hospital of St Nicholas. *"It reads, after translation, "Grant by Aldusa, widow of Henry (pistori [miller or baker]) [Gogeli] of Nantwich, to her son, John, chaplain, of a plot of land with buildings, courtyard and garden in Wycus Malbanus in the street of the hospital, bounded by the lane called Flowers Lane and the land of Robert son of Mark, and the high street and Flowerscroft; at an annual rent of two silver shillings to be paid to the lord of the fee, Richard Lewis [Junior], brother of Aldusa, for services and customs. Witnessed by lord Nicholas Ademet, dean of Nantwich and others. In 1325 Flowerscroft was known as Tenchersfield [History of Nantwich, James Hall, 1883, Page 6]."*

This as we will see again in the next chapter, directly relates to ***'The Rental of lands belonging to the Knights and Hospitallers of St. John of Jerusalem and of the lands of Robert Salamon, Nantwich area, c.1380-1390 (Cheshire Archives and Local Studies or CALS Ref: DDX350)'***, where we find Hugh le Mare rents one croft below (adjacent to) Fflowerslone from the Order of St John, i.e. the Hospitallers.

\* \* \* \* \* \* \*

Flowers Lane may have existed between St Nicholas' Hospital and the area of land which was known as 'Prestham'. This name derives from 'Priest's Ham', meaning an area of land or a farmstead, belonging to a priest(s). Prestham is presumed to have existed in Stapeley and Batherton, in the area to the immediate south and east of Brine Leas High School, next to Broad Lane which is now known as the Audlem Road.

'Prestham' is linked with Richard Marchumley, chaplain, who may be related to Robert de Marchumleye, the chaplain and Master of St Nicholas' Hospital around the 1320s. It is referred to in early 14$^{th}$ century deeds.

A brook ran north to south from Hospital Street to where the junction of the new A530 Peter De Stapleigh Way meets the A529 Audlem Road.

Flowers Lane may have run alongside this brook, to this once right-angled corner of the original Broad Lane, giving access between: the east of Nantwich, Hospital Street, and Millstone Lane; to the road to Audlem, and the area of land once known as 'Prestham'.

\* \* \* \* \* \* \*

A historic deed dating to c1307-1310, relates to Robert de Marchumleye, later one of the chaplains of St Nicholas', when he petitioned the King for redress (justice) because he had been assaulted whilst travelling, and was *"wounded to the point of death by wrongdoers":* Reynald Crump; Richard de Rodene; and Thomas Smute of Slepe [Sleap]. In the Petition are mentioned Upton Magna, Woore, and Sleap, all in Shropshire.[3]

According to two historic records dating to 1321, the Master of St Nicholas' Hospital at that time was called 'Adam del Hospital of Nantwich', and appeared as a witness to two leases for saltworks in Nantwich, which were held by Lilleshall Abbey.[4]

In two dispute records dated 17 December 1326, we are told that the Prior and Convent of St Thomas by Stafford, of the Order of St Augustine, claimed that the tithes of Aldelyme [Audlem] of which they held the parish church, and that both the lesser and greater tithes were despoiled, of tithes of [wheat] sheaves in a place commonly called Oxebruggehay, by Robert de Marchumley, Clerk (in holy orders), Keeper or Master of the Hospital of St Nicholas of Wych Malbane [Nantwich], William de Prayers, Priest, Richard de Dodington, Richard de Prayers and Ralph de Taylor, laymen.[5]

These historic records, therefore tell us that from 1326 until 1330, Robert de Marchumley was the Master and Chaplain of St

Nicholas' Hospital and Chapel. However, in 1321 there was also a Master of the Hospital called Adam.

A Grant likely dating to the mid 14th century, published from **'The "Domesday Roll" of Chester'**, in the **'Cheshire Sheaf'**, *"by Richard son of William son of Mathew and Beatrice his wife to William son of Mariot of a plot formerly belonging to [?] lord Nicholas Colfox chaplain, late [?] prior of the hospital of St. Nicholas of Wich Malbank, which he [Nicholas] bought from Adam de Berthon, between land of William Colfox and the road to the cemetery in the vill of Wych, rent 1d."*,[6] tells us another name of a Master and Chaplain of St Nicholas'. For more information on Nicholas Colfox, see later.

According to a record published in the **'Cheshire Sheaf'**, dating to 12 March 1364: we find the Appointment by the Bishop of [Lichfield] in Burton on Trent, of Nicholas Rivell, priest, to be granted to the Hospital or Chapel of St Nicholas of Namptwych, after a lapse of a hospital master for six months.[7]

Also according to a record published in the **'Cheshire Sheaf'**, dating to 20 April 1374, at Heywood [Staffordshire], *"John de Ormesheued, priest, was instituted to the chapel of the Hospital of St. Nicholas of Wici Malbani [Nantwich]"*, which was vacant on *""April 19[th] by the resignation of d[ominu]s/[Lord] Roger de Blakehurst at Chester, as appears by an instrument under the hand of Master John Barwe, at the presentation of Sir John Lovell, K[nigh]t, lord of Tichemersch".*[8]

A Grant dated 11 June 1374, of *"two places of land with their buildings in Wich Malbank, of which ... the other part of land lies in length between the high street and **the orchard of the Hospital of St. Nicholas**, and in width between the land which was that of Thomas Sharp on the one part and the land which William le Webb held of the aforesaid Robert [Fouleshurst of Edleston] at the time of this making on the other side".*[9]

This 1374 deed reveals that St Nicholas' Hospital had its own orchard.

According to the much later 1846 Tithe Map of Nantwich (CALS Ref: EDT 285/2), and its accompanying Apportionment, Plot 150, which existed behind Churche's Mansion (dating from 1577), was an orchard, owned by William Church Norcop, and tenanted by James Latham. This may have been part or most of the remnants of St Nicholas' Hospital Orchard, nearly 300 years after the hospital was dissolved.

In 1412, Alan Newark, who was the Master of the Hospital and Chapel of St Nicholas, left in his Will, 10 marks to the poor of Nantwich, for the benefit of the soul of the founder of his hospital.[10]

In an Appointment deed dated 12 May 1468: *"of land of a wich-house of 12 lead[pan]s in the Wich, between a street called le Wodestrete on the east, and the common cistern [drain] on the west, and between the land of Thomas son of John Wettenhall on the south, and land of the Hospital of St. Nicholas the Bishop on the north"*; we find that St Nicholas' Hospital held land near to the wich/salt houses in Wood Street, situated to the west of the River Weaver and on the north side of Welsh Row.[11]

In a Grant dated 24 August 1486: *"of land with its buildings lying in Wich Malbank between the King's high street leading towards Acton on the south side and the land of the Hospital of St. Nicholas on the north side, and between a certain lane called le Porteslone [Porch Lane, now known as Red Lion Lane, and next to the site of the ancient house known as the Porch House] on the east side and the land of Robert Fouleshurst, knight, on the west side"*; tells us that the Hospital held land to the north of Welsh Row, between Red Lion Lane and King's Lane, where the Fouleshursts had a Great Hall, located where the later Townsend House (since demolished) and its associated still surviving walled garden is situated.[12]

According to **'Notitia Cestriensis or Historical Notices of the Diocese of Chester, Rev. Francis Gastrell, Bishop of Chester (c1720), with notes by Rev. F. R. Raines, Volume I: Cheshire, The Chetham Society, First Series, Volume 8, 1845, Page 224'**, the Chantry and Hospital of St Nicholas was in existence in the early 14th century, and was also recorded in 1488/89, during the reign of Henry VII, and was an appurtenant (hereditary part) of the Barony, which was forfeited from Francis Lord Lovell after the battle of Stoke, and granted, inter alia (among other things), to Sir

William Stanley (chamberlain of Chester), the sixth part of the Barony of Wich-Malbank, and the advowson of the Chapel of St Nicholas, (and also the third part of the Chapel of St Lawrence).[13] This publication also tells us that *"the Hospital or Chantry is said to have been endowed by one of the Lords Lovell* with *the tithe proceeding from his lands"*.

In a 1489 Grant, we are told that: *"a messuage lying in Wich Malbank [Nantwich] in the high street leading towards the bridge on the east side of the said street, lately called le Bell, in length between the said street and land lately that of Richard Wildebore, and in width between land lately that of Hugh Wettenhall on the north side and land lately that of Thomas Stooke on the south side at the west end of the said messuage, and between land of the said Thomas Stooke on the north side and land of the Hospital of St. Nicholas and land of the heirs of William Glaseley on the south side"*; reveals that St Nicholas' Hospital held property near to the Bell Inn, which was a large coaching inn situated on the east side of Swine Market at the junction with High Street.[14]

A Grant dated 25 November 1494: *"of one half of a wich-house of 12 lead[pan]s lying in Wich Malbank between a certain street called le Wodestrete on the east, and the common cistern [drain] on the west, and between the land of Thomas son of John Wettenhall on the south, and the land of [the Hospital of] St. Nicholas the Bishop on the north"*; again tells us that the Hospital held property near Wood Street, to the west of the River Weaver, and to the north of Welsh Row.[15]

In an Inquisition [post mortem] (a local inquiry into the property, of what income and rights were due to the crown, and who the heir should be, after somebody's death) dating to 1529/30, in the reign of Henry VIII, on the forfeiture of Sir William Stanley, Knight, finds *"that he held the manor and vill of Wich Malbank in fee, with its appurtenances [hereditary lands] in Cow-lane, Newhall, Copenhale, Wolstanwood, and Acton, with the Chapel of St. Nicholas, and the third part of the Chapel of St. Lawrence"*.[16]

According to **'Nantwich: Saxon to Puritan, Eric Garton, 1972, Page 60'**, in a survey made in 1535, the Hospital of St Nicholas had a master named [William] Gwynne, and consisted of land and buildings worth £6, 11 shillings and 4 pence, annually. It also had tithes (a religious tax for its support, one tenth of people's annual produce or earnings) worth 13 shillings and 1¾ pence.

We are told in **'Inventories of Church Goods and Chantries in Cheshire, Temp Edward VI., The Historic Society of Lancashire and Cheshire, Volume 23 (1870-1872), Rev. Mackenzie E. C. Walcott, 27 January 1870, Page 179'**, that during the reign of Edward VI (1547-1553) the *"Frechapell of Sent Nicholas, was appraised at a yearly value of £7, 10 shillings, and that it was founded by the Lovell family"*.

This publication also tells us that at *"the Dissolution [of the Monasteries], William Hill, the Incumbent, had a pension of 100 s[hillings] a year for life, and was living in 1556"*.

However, as above stated, it is thought that the first baron of Nantwich, William Malbank, actually founded the hospital in 1083-4, and it was not founded later by the Lovell family. But rather they inherited the advowson of the Chapel and Hospital of St Nicholas, through one of the three female Malbank heirs.

St Nicholas' Chapel and Hospital was dissolved in 1548, but William Hill, its last chaplain, was paid his pension until 1561. It is believed at this time the hospital no longer had any silver plate, jewels, goods, ornaments, lead, or bells.

We find in a Sale deed dated 18 October 1569, that Richard Wrighte of Wiche Malbanke, alias Namptwiche, then sells to Roger Wilbram son of Rychard Wilbram, also of [Nant]Wich, *"all the tithes of flax, hemp, pigs and all other garden tithes arising in all houses, gardens and other tenements in the WICHE aforesaid, viz[namely] in the late hospitall of Sente Nicholas and all lands and tenements belonging to the same; all houses, gardens etc. on the south side of the Welshe Rowe, the South and west sides of the highe towne and the North side of the Milne strete, out of which the said late hospitall of St. Nicholas lately had/now hath/of right ought to have, two parts of the tithes of flax, hemp and pigs; to hold of the Queen as of her Manor of E[a]st Grenewiche (Co. Kent) in free socage"*.[17]

This historic deed tells us of the large property portfolio that the hospital owned, and its tithes in the town of Nantwich. We saw some of its holdings above, in various deeds too, and it certainly suggests a substantial income received for its upkeep and for the pilgrims, poor and ill it housed, or gave alms (charity) to.

In an Agreement dated 7 April 1654, between: William Peartree, Clerk, executor of John Thrush, late of Wich Malbanke, Gentleman, and John Farrar of Wich Malbanke, Shoemaker, one of the sons of John Farrar, Gentleman, deceased, late son in law of John Thrush; and Roger Wilbraham of Wich Malbanke, Esq[uire]; *"that William had assigned by an indenture dated 4 April 1654, to John Farrar the son, one croft with appurtenances [hereditary parts] called St Anns croft, late in the holding of John Thrush, for the residue of a term determinable on the decease of Roger Wilbraham of Darfould, Esq[uire], which is now in ar[r]ea[r]s of £55, 12s, 8d, for rent out of the said croft and other premises heretofore belonging to the Hospitall of St. Nicholas in Wich Malbanke, the reversion of which now belongs to Roger and his heirs, William and John Farrar, for the consideration money [initial cost of the lease] of £55, 12s, 8d, are agreed that Roger shall now hold the said croft, until the annual profits out of which he has received that sum".*[18]

This deed, therefore, gives us the later leaseholders of St Anne's Croft, which was situated to the south of Welsh Row Head, where Cartlake Close now exists, to the immediate east of the Shropshire Union Canal.

It also reveals that this field was once owned by St Nicholas' Hospital, and that may be why a 1555 Assignment of Lease refers to it as 'Seint Anne croft or hospital croft'.[19] It is shown on Joseph Fenna's Map of Nantwich 1794.

This field due to its name must have originally been held to augment the income of St Anne's Chapel, which was a small medieval chapel near to the crossing of the River Weaver, near the bridge on Welsh Row.

\* \* \* \* \* \* \*

In a Lease dated 25 December 1655, by Roger Wilbraham of Wiche Malbancke Esq[uire] to William Jackson of the same, tanner, we are told of *"a messuage/tenement and garden thereto adjoining with appurt[enance]s [hereditary parts] called St. Nicholas Hospitall in Wich Malbanke, now in the holding of the said William Jackson; for lives of the said William Jackson, Richard Jackson his son and William Steele, son of Thomas Steele of Cholmondeley, yeoman, at annual rent of £2-13-4; the lessee covenants at his own cost to erect a sufficient tanhouse on some part of the premises, to sink the necessary pits and to make 2 sufficient gates for the way leading to the said hospithall croft for the said Roger".*[20]

This 1655 deed reveals to us that part of the Hospital complex was replaced with the building of a tannery, which used to be situated between Churche's Mansion and the original site of the Sir Edmund Wright's Almshouses, at the end of Hospital Street and the beginning of London Road, on the south side of the road, and to the immediate east of Churche's Mansion, where the business 'Total Tools' now stands.

This tannery was associated with John Crewe, who lived at 'Hospital House', now known as 140-142 Hospital Street, and was a tanner. His famous son Ranulph Crewe bought the estate of Crewe Hall, previously the seat of the Fouleshursts, of Crewe and Barthomley, and built the magnificent Jacobean residence between 1615 and 1636.

A booklet dedicated to Nantwich's Tanneries is available from Nantwich Museum: **'Nantwich Tanneries, Andrew Lamberton and Glynn Skerratt, 2020'**.

There was also a public house, which is believed to date back to 1767, named 'The Bull's Head',[21] and was situated to the immediate east of the original site of Sir Edmund Wright's Almshouses. They were built in 1638, and on the opposite side of London Road, to the car park of The Leopard public house. The Almshouses and Bull's Head; may too be built on land which was originally part of the Chapel and Hospital of St Nicholas.

Also next to Sir Edmund Wright's Almshouses, at their original site, was a field called 'Almshouse Meadow'. Another Alms-house Meadow was annexed to the Wilbraham's Almshouses which stood at the end of Welsh Row, on the other side of the town.

The 1655 deed also tells us that William Jackson, *"shall sinke a pitt to receave the filthe w[hi]ch might be noxious to the watercourse runninge alonge the west side of the Hospithall croft orotherwyse to devert the nysome? water that shall come from any of his said pitts soe as not to be preduditiall at any tyme to the said watercourse."* This therefore tells us that the field known as the 'Hospital Croft' was to the east of a stream which is shown on the c.1875 Ordnance Survey Map, as running from the north-west to the south-east and to the rear of the Tannery site, and to the west of another watercourse which meets the former, and acted as the township boundary.

Interestingly the 1846 Tithe Map shows a trackway running to the immediate west of the former watercourse, as well as another trackway running southward from London Road to the east of the original site of the 'Wrights Almshouses'. Could these be the rights of way, William Jackson had to provide gates for? The plot on the Tithe Map is known as No. 151 'Croft', and was most likely originally the 'Hospital Croft'.

*140-142 Hospital Street or 'Hospital House'*

The above 1655 deed certainly proves that the hospital was situated here, like the tradition that the hospital buildings stood on or near to the house now known as 140-142 Hospital Street, which James Hall in his **'A History of the Town and Parish of Nantwich or Wych-Malbank, Cheshire, 1883 (Republished 1972)'**, tells us was known as 'Hospital House', and the once home of the Crewe family.

The 1655 deed also includes that it was a *"Counterpart of a Lease of* **ye Hospitall Howse** *to Will[iam] Jackson for 99 years determinable upon 3 Lives for £2, 13s, 4d Rent"* on the reverse. It also tells us that *"Will[iam] Jackson ye Leasser dyed ye beginning of ye year 1697"*.[22]

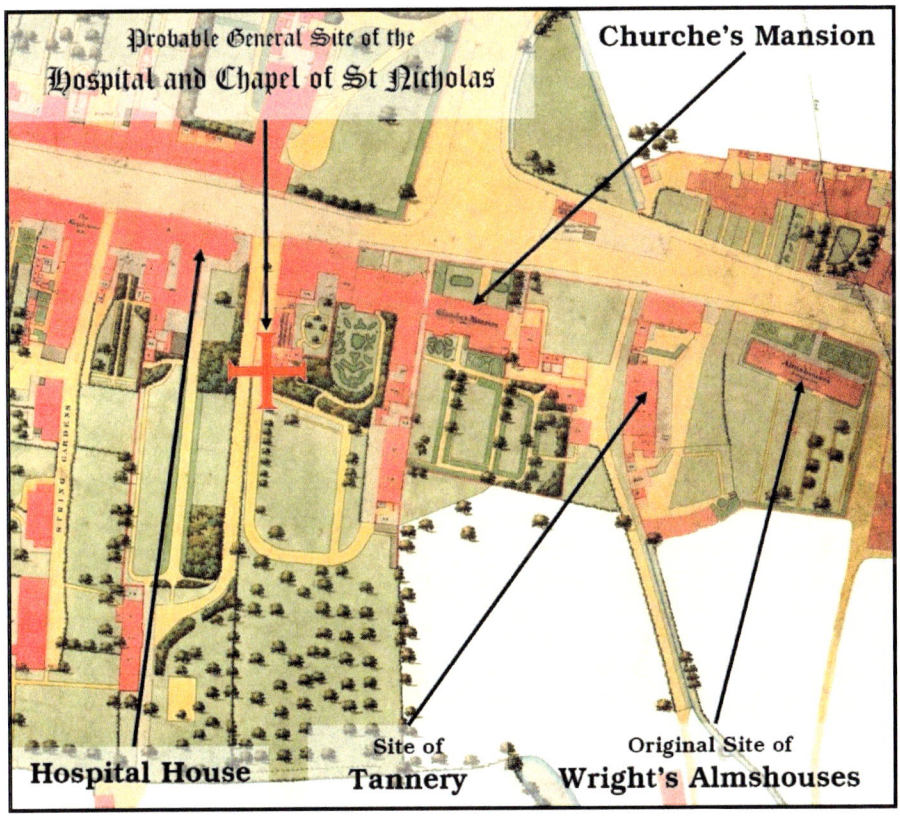

***Probable Location of the Hospital and Chapel of St Nicholas, Extract from the Board of Health Town Plan: Nantwich, 1851***

Stone remains were discovered in the garden of the 'Hospital House' during 19th century building works, whilst taking down an old chimney stack, and gate posts, with stone balls upon, at the east end of the house, and erecting a new extension.

The stones were identified by Thomas Bower, Architect, who lived at the house during the building works, as being the capital and base of a Norman Romanesque doorway, which may have been all that was left of the medieval hospital.[23]

Could the gate-posts with stone balls upon, at the east end of 'Hospital House' have been one of the gates which had to be made for the way leading to the hospital croft, we saw in the Lease dated 25 December 1655, above?

Dr [John] Turner, who also lived at 140-142 Hospital Street, told us in a letter published in **'The Nantwich Chronicle, Saturday 4 June 1938, Page 5'**, that the *"old stones discovered by Mr. Bower [were then] still in the garden."*

It is not known where these stones can be found now.

* * * * * * *

Interestingly, the Hospital of St Nicholas is recorded as being a free chapel at the time of the Dissolution, and was not part of the control of an associated monastery nor controlled by the Church and its bishops.

St Nicholas' Hospital is thought to have been associated with the 'Order of Knights of the Hospital of Saint John of Jerusalem', or as we know them the Knights Hospitaller, who held quite a few properties in the town of Nantwich according to rental documents (see later).

The Hospitallers held the island of Rhodes, and their medieval fortress there had a chapel dedicated to St Nicholas, which the fortress was named after. Fort Ricasoli in Malta had a chapel dedicated to St Nicholas too, but was built later between 1696 and 1698, by the Order of St John.

There is also a St Nicholas Chapel at Temple Church, Bristol, which was originally a Templar foundation, which was later inherited by the Hospitallers.

It was standard practice to include chapels in their fortifications, and often the fortress was named after the chapel it housed.

Sometimes these chapels were named after members' saintly namesakes by the Hospitaller hierarchy who founded them.

St Nicholas was born in the village of Patara in Asia Minor, during the 4$^{th}$ century AD. He was the patron saint of sailors and was held in great esteem by those going on Crusade, due to their long journey usually by ship to the Holy Land.

In times of danger, people of Faith, would turn to him to perform wonders and miracles, including controlling the winds and seas, subduing storms, and defeating evil. He was sometimes known as 'The Lord of the Sea'.

He became Bishop of Myra, today in Turkey, but during the Roman persecution of Christians, he was imprisoned and tortured. Later after being released, he died in Myra around 345AD.

He was also the patron saint of merchants, archers, repentant thieves, prostitutes, children, brewers, pawnbrokers, unmarried people, and students. He was also known as St Nicholas of Myra or Bari, and became Santa Claus, from the tradition that he gave secret gifts.

The House of the Knights of Malta, in the old town of Bitetto in the Metropolitan city of Bari, southern Italy, is associated with the Hospitallers. St Nicholas' remains were enshrined in the 'Basilica di San Nicola' in Bari, after the Saracens took Myra, now in Turkey (which was originally in Greece), where his original shrine was located, and from where his relics were transferred.

This, as well as being a patron saint of sailors, made a strong link between St Nicholas, the Crusaders, and of course the Hospitallers.

The city of Myra was a place where the medieval pilgrims and Crusaders travelling by horse or foot, stayed on the way from Italy to Palestine, so St Nicholas would have been strong in their faithful minds, even if they didn't travel by ship.

He was also very much revered in Malta, with a cult growing up around him, most likely due to it being an island where the Crusader ships would have been harboured. They also took haven on the more easterly island of Cyprus, and the island of Sicily to the north, as well as Crete and Rhodes, also to the east, whilst they made their way by sea to the Holy Land.

Bari, Malta, and Sicily were strongholds of the Normans, so it is possible, like Eric Garton tells us below, that William Malbank the first baron of Nantwich may have travelled to the Holy Land, via these places, and had come across the veneration of St Nicholas.

This may be the reason why he set up Nantwich's first hospital dedicated to the saint, and why it is linked with the Knights Hospitaller in the first place.

St Nicholas was also the dedication of other medieval hospitals in the UK. Those include:-

- Harbledown (Canterbury), Kent (for lepers, established c1084 and founded by Archbishop Lanfranc);
- Canterbury, Kent (St Nicholas and St Katherine; first recorded in 1293, and founded by W. Cokyn);
- Ospringe, Kent (first recorded in 1241);
- Rochester (Whiteditch), Kent (hospital for lepers, first recorded in 1253);
- Hornchurch (Havering), Essex (Saints Nicholas and Bernard; first recorded in 1159, and founded by Henry II);
- Lewes (Westout), East Sussex (for the infirmed poor, first mentioned in circa 1085, and founded by W. De Warenne with the patronage of the Priory);
- Bury St Edmunds (without Eastgate), Suffolk (first mentioned in circa 1215);
- Portsmouth, Hampshire (God's House or St John the Baptist and St Nicholas; first recorded in 1224, and founded by Peter des Roches, Bishop);

- Salisbury (Harnham Bridge), Wiltshire (for poor, sick and infirmed travellers, first recorded in 1214, and founded by the Bishop, Dean and Chapter of Salisbury);
- Royston, Hertfordshire (hospital for lepers, first recorded in 1213, and founded by Ralph);
- Spalding, Lincolnshire (hospital for lepers, first recorded in 1313);
- Newport, Shropshire (first recorded in 1446, and founded by W. Glover, etc., of the Town);
- Chesterfield, Derbyshire (first recorded in 1276);
- Clitheroe, Lancashire (hospital for lepers, first recorded in 1211, and founded by the Town);
- Carlisle, Cumbria (for lepers, poor and sick, established 1199 or earlier, founded by the King, and the Crown and the Priory were patrons);
- Appleby, Cumbria (hospital for lepers, first recorded before 1240, and Shap Abbey is patron);
- Richmond, North Yorkshire;
- Pickering, North Yorkshire;
- and St Andrew's, Fife, Scotland (for lepers, established in the late 12$^{th}$ century).

(**Main Source: *'The Medieval Hospitals of England, Rotha Mary Clay, 1909'*).**

\* \* \* \* \* \* \*

The Templars were also thought to have held some property in Nantwich, but it is difficult to separate their holdings, from that of the Hospitallers.

The Knights Templar were locally based at Keele Chapel and Preceptory, in North Staffordshire. They owned property in the area, which was transferred after the Order was suppressed and dissolved in the early 14$^{th}$ century, to the Hospitallers.

The dedication of St Nicholas to the Chapel and Hospital, as stated above, does in fact suggest a Hospitaller foundation, because other chapels and churches associated with them carried this dedication, albeit not as widespread as those of St John the Baptist.

Also, both Orders never had priests in charge of their chapels, but rather chaplains, who were not controlled by the Church or its bishops, which this hospital also had for its described free chapel.

It is also possible and has been suggested by others, that the Malbanks especially the first Baron, William, may have been involved in the Crusades, and even travelled to the Holy Land, or at least granted land to one or both Orders of the Templars or Hospitallers, because we know they both held property in the town of Nantwich, as well as in its hundred (an administrative division of a larger region), and the hundreds adjacent to it.

There are also three stone knights or crusader tombs located in the North Transept of St Mary's Church in Nantwich, and another, defaced, built into the South Transept's eastern wall, behind the organ.

Sometimes medieval hospitals were transferred or given as a gift to the Hospitallers or other military religious orders, like land also was, especially if giving support to the Crusades, or if a benefactor was actually taking part in the Crusades.

This is also claimed by Eric Garton, in **'Nantwich: Saxon to Puritan, A History of the Hundred of Nantwich, 1050 to 1642, 1972, Pages 2-3'**:-

> "The earliest Nantwich charter which is dated is of the year 1114 AD and shows that the first baron and Roger de Wiccadest had granted land to the Prior and Brothers of the Hospital of St. John of Jerusalem at a date earlier than 1114. The charter is in Latin and the translation reads (1: Additional Charters 43371.); "GRANT by Brother Alan, Prior of the Brothers of the Hospital of Jerusalem in England, with the consent of the chapter, to Edith, daughter of Ludovic, of land which they (the Knights) had in the village of Nantwich by gift of William Malbedeng and Roger de Wiccadest, for an annual rent of two shillings. And in return Edith gives up all claim to her land her father, Ludovic, held from the Hospital of Jerusalem." Witnessed by the Brothers of the Order on the feast of St. Martin, 1114.

*This was just 12 months after the Pope had recognised the Order of the Knights Hospitallers, which had come into being in Jerusalem about the year 1099 after the Hospital at Jerusalem had been destroyed about a hundred years earlier. It is possible William Malbedeng (or Malbanc) and Roger de Wiccadest took part in a Crusade to the Holy Land about 1099 and benefited from the services of the Hospitallers and made the grant of land in Nantwich for that reason. At least, this is what many Crusaders did on their return to their homes. Neither William Malbanc nor Roger de Wiccadest are included in the records of the Order as members of it."*

This may mean that St Nicholas' Hospital which William Malbank was believed to have founded in 1083-4, may have soon after, been gifted to the Hospitallers, by him.

We also know that Ralph Sarazin gave to the Prior and brethren of the Hospital [of St John of Jerusalem], i.e. the Hospitallers, in 1316-17, a salt house in Wich Malbank, which belonged to William de la Bach, which he conceded in 1309-10 the same to Hugh Fouleshurst, by payment of 13 shillings and 4 pence per annum. (Woodnoth Collections in Dodsworth Manuscripts, xxxi. Folio 144 (Bodleian Library)).

This historic deed tells us that Ralph Sarazin, possibly a Saracen who had helped the Crusaders, and had come to settle in Nantwich, gave a salt house to the Prior and brethren of the Hospital, which the Knights Hospitaller were sometimes known as, and tells us that they too held salt houses in the town.

We also know from my history **'The Lost Chapel and the Pubs of Barthomley, Charles E. S. Fairey, 2019 (Rev 2020)'**, which was published online on my historian website, as a free ebook; that the Hospitallers had a Chapel in Barthomley, as well as a Chapel dedicated to St John the Baptist in Kinderton, and also that they held court in the town of Middlewich.

It seems likely that at least in its early history as well as later history, the Hospital of St Nicholas on Hospital Street, in the town of Nantwich; was actually controlled by the Hospitallers; and it might be that they too had had a court in the town of Nantwich.

They held quite a lot of land and property in Cheshire, far more than the Templars, whose estates they inadvertently largely inherited after the suppression of that Order in the early 14th century.

We are also told on page 708 of **'Magna Britannia; Being a Concise Topographical Account of the Several Counties of Great Britain, Volume II: Cambridgeshire and Cheshire, Daniel and Samuel Lysons, 1810'**, that there was *"an estate within this barony [Nantwich], called St. John of Jerusalem's fee, having belonged to the knights hospitallers of St. John of Jerusalem."* This may directly relate to the Barony of Nantwich, of which they held properties in the town (as we'll see later) or to their holdings in the whole of Nantwich Hundred.

Allan Whatley in **'Buildings in Nantwich, Spring 1995'** includes that St Nicholas' Hospice, was also known as St 'John's', obviously referring to the 'Order of Knights of the Hospital of **Saint John** of Jerusalem'.

Another deed may be linked with the Hospitallers in the town too, because a Grant by *"William of Poole to Richard son of Robert Coterel of Poole (later 13th century?) of [a pound of?] cumin [an aromatic spice] which I had of the Hospital [of St John of Jerusalem] in the vill of Wich Malbank each year in [...] street"*, records. (CALS Ref: DMW 6/27).[24]

The Hospitallers also owned and ran St Lazarus' Leper Hospital in Burton upon Trent in Staffordshire.

* * * * * * *

# The Knights Hospitaller and Nantwich

The 'Order of Knights of the Hospital of Saint John of Jerusalem', or Knights Hospitaller for short, were a religious military order, founded to provide care for sick, poor, or injured pilgrims visiting the Holy Land, and much like the more famous 'Knights Templar' held vast estates throughout Europe, to raise revenue for the Order. Like the Templars, they also fought in the many battles against the Saracens for the Holy Land.

The Hospitallers are believed to have originally been founded or descended from a group who created a hospital dedicated to St John the Baptist, in the city of Jerusalem. Although there is some dispute to their original founding and date, it is largely believed this hospital began in the early 11$^{th}$ century, and by the 1070s or 1080s, they had become a religious Order. Here they cared for the sick, poor, and injured pilgrims, coming to the Holy Land. The Hospitallers certainly existed when the Crusaders conquered Jerusalem in 1099, and were officially recognised by the Pope in 1113. They later became a military order of knights, still caring for the sick, but also defending the faithful.

After the Templars were arrested in England in 1308, after King Edward II delayed an instruction from the Pope, most of the Templar's lands and assets by 1314, or soon afterwards, were inherited by the Knights Hospitaller.

They were also sometimes known as the 'Order of the Priory of the Hospital of St John [the Baptist] of Jerusalem' and as the 'Monastery / Priory of St John of Jerusalem', or simply as the 'Priory' or 'Order of St John'.

The Hospitallers held lands and properties in Nantwich.[25] After the Reformation but based on their old estates, the only property in Nantwich they held was a messuage (a house, outbuildings and land) in Hospital Street.[26] They also held properties and saltpits in Middlewich.[27] After the Reformation but based on their old estates, in Middlewich they held: four salthouses; eleven messuages; ten burgages (town houses); and a garden.[28] In 1270 Thomas son of Peter de Warinhull, held saltworks in Middlewich, as tenants of the Hospital of St John of Jerusalem, for a fine of 3 marks, and an annual reserved rent of 3 shillings and 10 pence, due to the Hospital each Michaelmas.[29] As well as properties and four saltpits in Northwich, in c1206.[30] After the Reformation, but based on their old estates, those properties in Northwich were: a messuage; three salthouses, and a tenement (a dwelling often with outbuildings and land).[31]

Around Nantwich they also held: a Grange (a large farm belonging to a religious house) at (Church) Minshull,[32] and four acres of land, held in socage (rent or service) by David Dod of Leighton, in Church Coppenhall,[33] land at Elton and Moston, near Sandbach; land at Wardle,[34] given to them by Simon Tuschet and Matthew of Newton, in 1171-73,[35] and part of the manor of Ridley during the reign of Edward I (1272-1307).[36]

The Hospitallers also had a small estate or camera with a medieval chapel, at Barthomley, to the east of Nantwich. This chapel existed until the 16th century Reformation. Please see **'The Lost Chapel and the Pubs of Barthomley, Charles E. S. Fairey, 2019 (Rev 2020)'** (Available as a free ebook @ https://sites.google.com/site/charlesfaireyhistorian/).

In the above publication, we find that the Praers and the Fulleshurst families were lords of Barthomley, and that branches of those families also lived and held estates in and around Nantwich, as well as being prominent lordly families of the town.

* * * * * * *

***'The Rental of lands belonging to the Knights and Hospitallers of St. John of Jerusalem and of the lands of Robert Salamon, Nantwich area, c.1380-1390 (CALS Ref: DDX350)'***, tells us: the current tenant(s) at that time; the type of property; the previous tenant(s); and the income due; in and around Nantwich:-

### Rent roll of [the Knights Hospitaller of] St John [of Jerusalem]

- John the Maisterson (Master's Son) for land in Cus[tard]? crofts which had been Alice the daughter of Robert / of Stapeley_6 d
  *(Note: There is a Custard Croft north of Beam Street, at the end of Dog Lane, on Joseph Fenna's 1794 Map)*

- Hugh the Mare for one croft below Flowers lane_12 d
  *(Note: Flowerslone or Floureslane is a lost Street Name, mentioned by J. McN. Dodgson in **'The Place-names of Cheshire, Volume XLVI, Part III, Page 35 & 40'**, and is linked with 'Flourescroft' in Nantwich)(It is believed to have existed next to St Nicholas' Hospital)*

- Thomas the Maisterson for a House and Garden which had been Margaret the Hoys / and William Marriot_3 d

- Lord [Sir] Richard Cradock, Knight, for land which had been Richard Girdy_8 d
  *(Note: Sir Richard Cradock, Knight, was the heir of Sir David Cradock, Knight, whose alabaster effigy still stands inside the South Transept of St Mary's Church, Nantwich)*

- Roger Hancock for all of his lands and tenements (dwellings often with outbuildings and land)_4 s 4 d

- Eleanor the Fyesher for land and a tenement which had been Roger the son of Rondulph_1 d

- John Twoyerold for land and a tenement which had been Elizabeth of Cholmondeley_3 d

- Rick Cromp for land and a tenement which had been Hugh of Fouleshurst_12 d

- Henry Cromp for land and a tenement which had been Robert Tomgrene_6 d

- Thomas the Maisterson for one messuage (house with land and ancillary buildings) which had been Hamon of Ray / Bufford_4 d

- Thomas the Maisterson for one croft which had been Adam the Carter and Margaret his wife_12 d

- Matilda the Small for_2 d

- for one croft in Horepull that named Keep? crofts_12 d
  *(Note: Horpull is the name of a lost place in Poole, known as 'Warpoole', to the north of Nantwich, and thought to derive from 'Hoare Poole', i.e. Grey or Boundary Pool. It is mentioned by J. McN. Dodgson in **'The Place-names of Cheshire, Volume XLVI, Part III, Page 149'**)*

## Rent roll of Robert Salamon

- William Dawson for one garden which had been William the Smith_5 d
- Thomas the Goldsmith for one Garden which had been Richard Hulsone_4 d
- Thomas the Goldsmith for one messuage with a garden and land in the Wall / Field with a garden below the Wall_20 d in oil
  *(Note: The Wall Fields are shown on Joseph Fenna's 1794 Map of Nantwich as existing where Manor Road exists today, north of Beam Street)*
- Urian de Egerton / for one messuage with a garden_6 d
  *(Note: David son of Urian of Egerton is mentioned in a 1340-1 Deed relating to Cheshire; and Urian de Egerton appears in Deeds in the 1370s in Cheshire)*
- Urian de Egerton for one Garden / that named the ...?yard_12 d?
- William de Hanley for a messuage and a garden_1 d
- Robert de Fouleshurst for land and a tenement which had been John Judland?_2 s 1 d
- Maude the Small for the leased properties_15 d and one share [?] of beer/bread?
- Maude the Small for one messuage in Dog Lane_1 d
  *(Note: Doglone or Dog Lane is a Nantwich Street Name, mentioned by J. McN. Dodgson in **'The Place-names of Cheshire, Volume XLVI, Part III, Page 33'**, and was first mentioned according to the book in 1467. This deed dates to circa 1380-90, so means the lane dates to an earlier period still. This lane still exists to the north of Beam Street, and to the north-west of Nantwich Bus Station, and to the immediate right of the 'Bench Bistro and Bar' once known as 'The Shakespeare' public house)*
- William de Spurstowe for one messuage [?] which had been John Bleynstoke_1 oil
- John son of Richard the Mayre for the Wall Yard?_5 s 1 d 1 in oil
- And one messuage between Beam Street (one of the main streets in Nantwich)_1 d and 12 oaken based pitchers together
- Item Nicholas Colfox for land and a tenement which had been Richard de Whitmore_15 d and 12 oaken based pitchers together
  *(Note: Nicholas Colfox appears as a witness in some Medieval Nantwich Deeds)*

*(**Note**: This Medieval Latin document was translated by me with help from Linda Briggs (Nantwich Museum Research Group), and Caroline Picco (Cheshire Archives & Local Studies)).*

The Rent Roll of Robert Salamon being included with the Knights of St John, or the Hospitallers, most likely means he was linked with the Order, and part of its hierarchy.

\* \* \* \* \* \* \*

In a **'Copie of an old Rental of the Commandery of Ivelie in the Countie of Chester formerly belonging to the Knights Hospitallers of St. John of Jerusalem in England. Harleian Manuscript, MS 1999, Entry 6, 18.a, (Folios 21r-30v), Catalogue of the Harleian Manuscripts in the British Museum, Volume II, 1808, MS 1999, Entry 6, 18.a, Page 379'**, which is in Latin, and dates to between 1600 and 1640 (deduced from the names included in the ten-page list), tells us that the following property was held by the Hospitallers:-

- *"Katherine Wrighte, Widow, for a messuage in The Hospital Street in the town of Malbank_ 2 s."*

The same rental survey also tells us: the holder(s); the type of property; where it is; the tenant(s); and the income due; around Nantwich:-

- *"George Vernon, Esquire, for two messuages in Coppenhall in the tenure of William Malbon_ 11s 8d;*
- *Sir Richard Wilbr[ah]am, Knight, for a messuage in the same place in the tenure of Randall Cliffe_ 3d;*
- *George Vernon, Esquire, for a messuage in Church Coppenhall in the tenure of Thomas Lea_ 6d;*
- *The heirs of John Widenburie for a messuage in Bridgemere in the tenure of ... Raynshowe_ 2s;*
- *Sir William Brereton, Knight, for a messuage in Alsager in the tenure of Robert Gallie_ 12d;*
- *Lady Mary Cholmondlie for a messuage in Alsager in the tenure of Robert Gallie_ 6d;*
- *George Manwaringe for a messuage in Poole Cross in the tenure of Robert Harcotte_ 3d;*

- *... Minshill of the Rectory of Minshull for one parcel of land in Minshull sometime in the tenure of John Tottye_4d."*

The John Tottye mentioned in the last record was probably associated with Totty's Hall, which was originally a small manor house with a gatehouse, which was located just to the north of Leighton Brook, to the west of Minshull New Road (which was originally called Dodd's Lane), in Leighton, to the north west of Crewe. The site of Totty's Hall has been developed but sadly was not fully investigated, archaeologically.

The Hospitaller properties around Nantwich recorded above other than in the town itself were: three messuages in Coppenhall; a messuage in Church Coppenhall; a messuage in Bridgemere; two messuages in Alsager; and a messuage in Poole (Cross). They also held the manor of Ridley.[37]

\* \* \* \* \* \* \*

The Hospitallers' Barthomley Chapel no longer existed by the lease of Booth's Cottage in Barthomley, in 1569, which was built on or near to its site, so does not appear in this early 17th century Rental Survey.

\* \* \* \* \* \* \*

In **'The manor of Iveley, Cheshire with rights etc. appurtenant, late in the possession of Charles Stuart, late king of England, & part of the See of St. John of Jerusalem, as surveyed by a commission, set up by Parliament, for sale of the honours, manors & lands, previously belonging to the king, queen & prince, 13 page survey & rental, 1650 (CALS Ref: DLT/A37/1)'**, which is in English, tells us that the following property was held by the Hospitallers in Nantwich, much the same as the above, i.e.:-

- *"Katherine Wright, for a Messuage in ye Hospitall streete in Le [the] vico [town of] Malbano al[ia]s Namptwich_2 s."*

\* \* \* \* \* \* \*

The messuage held by Katherine Wright(e), in the above two surveys dating to the early to mid 17th century, is likely to be the

Hospital and Chapel of St Nicholas, and if so, proves it was held ultimately by the Hospitallers.

Katherine Wright of Wich Malbank was the widow of Richard Wright, and their heirs were their daughters, Elizabeth and Margaret Wright.

Richard Wright of the Bell Inn held the lands: of St Nicholas' Hospital; St Lawrence's Hospital, as well as being the Chapel of St Lawrence's last Chaplain; and the Guildhall in the Churchyard; after the Dissolution.

He also held properties of the dissolved Abbey of Combermere.[38]

\* \* \* \* \* \* \*

Eric Garton, in **'Nantwich: Saxon to Puritan, A History of the Hundred of Nantwich, 1050 to 1642, 1972, Pages 2-3'**: also tells us that a Charter (Ref: Additional Charters 43371) which is undated, and is a certificate by Brother Godard that *"the Widow, Beatrix, had before him many others in the court of St. John, given proof of holding lands in Wicus (Nantwich), which Bernard held from the Knights Hospitallers."*

\* \* \* \* \* \* \*

The Hospitallers estates in Cheshire were controlled from their important commandery / preceptory (like a large grange farm, with manor house and church / chapel) at Yeaveley (Iveley in the records) in Derbyshire. This commandery was later annexed with Barrow near Burton on Trent, in the early 15th century.

We are also told in an account of the possessions of the late monasteries in Cheshire, dating between 25 July 1555 and 5 July 1558, during the Reformation, that it included an account of the possessions of the [Knights Hospitaller's] Preceptory of Yeveley [in Derbyshire], where its Cheshire estates were ruled from.[39] Sadly the document doesn't include all their holdings, just a generic description.

They may also have at some point subordinately controlled some of their Cheshire estates from within the City of Chester. Their supposedly most important properties within the City (although far from verified for certain as Knights Hospitaller entities, and it is hotly contested if they were linked at all), were located: just outside the Northgate, at the Hospital of St John of Jerusalem which was replaced by the Little Church of St John (which was founded by Ranulph de Blondeville of Chester); and from part of the large St John's Church or Priory which contained a hospital of the Order (once attached to the East End of the Church), by the Amphitheatre. They did however definitely hold quite a few other properties within the City in Northgate Street, Eastgate Street, beyond the Eastgate, Foregate Street, Cow Lane, Spittle Field, Chester Field, Flookersbrook, Broadhey, Banckfield, etc.[40]

However the Knights Templar Preceptory and Church at Keele, Staffordshire, and its estates, including the camerae or small estate, with Chapel, at Onneley, which was granted sometime after the dissolution of the Templars, to the Hospitallers in 1324, was controlled from their Commandery at Halston, near Whittingham, near Ellesmere in Shropshire. Their Chapel at the Halston Hall Estate, still exists, and is only one of two timber-framed churches left in Shropshire.

By the time of the Tudor Dissolution, much of the rental income of the now dissolved Order of Knights of the Hospital of Saint John of Jerusalem, or the Knights Hospitaller for short, became the property of local gentry or the crown, who inherited their estates. However due to the sums hardly changing from the earlier medieval period, and the unceasing decrease in the value of money, the rental incomes were hardly worth the expense of collection.

Many of the properties in Cheshire, and specifically Nantwich, as well as that due for 'Hospitelerscroft' in Barthomley, a yearly rental of only 12 pence was due to the Knights Hospitaller, or those who inherited their estates after the Dissolution, so that by the late 16th and the 17th century, it was hardly worth the cost of collecting.

\* \* \* \* \* \* \*

It was not uncommon for members of the nobility to take part in the Crusades in the Holy Land, and many gave land to the Templars and Hospitallers, as gifts to support the Crusades. This gave those military religious orders much-needed revenue for their exploits in the Holy Land.

For example: Henry de Audley founded the Abbey of Hulton in 1223, on lands adjacent to a holding owned by the Templars at the Keele Preceptory and Church, and the Audleys Red Castle, near Whitchurch, is home to legends of the Templars, never mind the Holy Grail, and whose family was originally and at length based at Audley, and Heighley Castle, near to Barthomley; Bertram de Verdun founded the Abbey of Croxden, in 1176, who was known as a Crusader, and had lands in both North Staffordshire and South Cheshire; and Ranulph de Blondeville of Chester founded the Abbey of Dieulacres, at Poulton first, which was then moved near to Leek, in 1214, who was also a known Crusader, and who constructed Beeston Castle, which is thought to have been based upon Crusader Castles in the Holy Land; Ranulphus de Allsacher [Alsager] also gave land at Bircheley to Dielacres Abbey, and was one of its benefactors.

* * * * * * *

There are thought to be three medieval Crusader or knight grave slabs located in St George's Chapel in the North Transept of St Mary's Church in Nantwich.

Two are freestanding on either side of the main altar: with flowery octagonal cross motifs, atop a central rod; and another is partially hidden by the left-hand grave slab, set into the floor in an east-west alignment, with some carved details discernible, including the flowery octagonal cross motif to the top, and the rod of the cross running towards the west.

The Octagon and the Number 8 are spiritually representative of the End of the World and Judgement, as well as the Last or Eighth Day, referring to the Eternal Day in Heaven.

There is another Crusader-type grave slab, albeit defaced, built into the north-eastern wall of the South Transept behind the organ.[41]

These tomb stones once likely belonged to Hospitaller Knights, who either had lived in Nantwich or nearby, and who may have served in the Holy Land. These give us a valuable tangible link to the religious military Order and the past.

Also according to **'The History of Cheshire, Volume 3, George Ormerod, 1882, Page 445'**, there was another Crusader-type grave slab in the church, because we are told that *"near the south door, is a coffin-shaped slab, with a cross thereon, ornamented with oak leaves springing from the shaft. The head is formed by four oak leaves conjoined within a circle. It most probably relates to some members of the Order of St. John of Jerusalem, who had lands here."*

James Hall in his **'History of Nantwich, 1883, Page 319'**, tells us that this grave slab was moved to the churchyard, and sited under a young birch tree, and that there were other flat stones removed from inside the church to the churchyard.

*The Three Crusader or Knights Hospitaller Grave Stones located in St George's Chapel, in the North Transept, St Mary's Church, Nantwich*

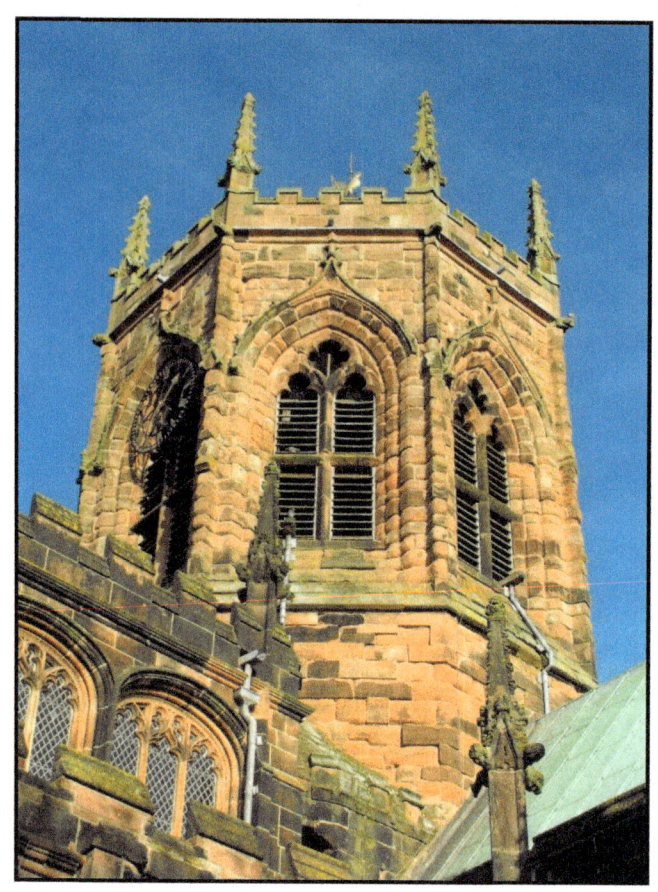

**Nantwich Church's Octagonal Tower**

Interestingly, St Mary's Church has a late 14th century Octagonal Tower, which is a rare feature in the UK, and reminiscent of: the flowery octagonal cross motifs on the Crusader Tombstones; the Dome of the Rock on Temple Mount in Jerusalem; which along with the Church of the Holy Sepulchre, also in the holy city, became a model for the round Templar churches which stood throughout medieval Europe.

Good examples of Templar round churches may be seen at: Temple in London; Garway in Herefordshire, albeit mainly rebuilt over by a Hospitaller Church, with just the footings remaining, and part of the Chancel arch wall; and at Ludlow Castle, where a round chapel dedicated to St Mary Magdalene, stands, with two

Templar Crosses carved into one of the arch capital's of the canopies above the seats revolving around the interior of the round nave.[42]

The Dome of the Rock which is an early medieval mosque was made into a church when Jerusalem was captured by the Crusaders in 1099. It was believed by the Templars to be on the site of King Solomon's Temple, and its Holy of Holies. The Dome of the Rock or 'Templum Domini' (Temple of the Lord) as it was known to the Crusaders, was often depicted on the seals of the Grand Masters of the Knights Templar. Although it has octagonal outer walls, it has a circular arcade of columns and piers to its central interior, which is topped by its circular dome. The nearby Al-Aqsa Mosque also became the headquarters of the Templars, during the 12$^{th}$ century.

Similar medieval octagonal towered churches exist at: St Mary's Church, Stafford, with a lower square and upper octagonal tower, which originally had a spire to its top; St Nicholas' Church, Grosmont in Monmouthshire, albeit with a spire on top, but with a square four column base, much like Nantwich, which also has Hospitaller or Templar grave slabs; Ely Cathedral in Cambridgeshire, although a lantern central tower, but also with a western octagonal tower; and St Mary's Church, Pakenham in Suffolk.

Interestingly for this study, we find that in 1353, Edward the Black Prince, as Earl of Chester, marched with Henry of Grosmont, who was the Duke of Lancaster, to Cheshire and the City of Chester, to protect the justices who were holding assizes, and took a great deal of money from them, seizing properties. This gives a direct link to Cheshire and Monmouthshire, and the churches of Nantwich and Grosmont, and their similar octagonal towers, as well as their shared dedication to St Nicholas; albeit Nantwich's most likely originally having a chantry chapel dedicated to him, rather than the later main dedication of the Church to both St Mary and St Nicholas.

St Nicholas' at Grosmont is also a cruciform church with its central octagonal tower (with a spire on top), and is sometimes known as a 'miniature cathedral'.

Another octagonal tower exists at Grand-Sauve Abbey in La Sauve near to the city of Bordeaux in France. With Richard II being born at Bordeaux, and Sir David Cradock, his friend, being made the Mayor of Bordeaux, and being involved in the Hundred Years' War (1337-1453), like many other Cheshire nobles, the link between Bordeaux and Nantwich is a strong one too (see later details).

This may infer along with the Hospitaller link and the Grosmont and/or Bordeaux connection, another reason why Nantwich's St Mary's has an octagonal tower.

* * * * * * *

It is likely along with the reputed founder of Nantwich's 14th century St Mary's, Sir David Cradock,[43] (see later), and a mysterious Guild or Brotherhood of the Holy Cross, that the Hospitallers gave funds towards the building of the Church of Nantwich; as well as its royal benefactors (see below).

# Sir Nicholas Colfox, Knight and Chaplain
# Friend of King Richard II
# Prior of the Hospital of St Nicholas

The following historic deed tells us that lord Nicholas Colfox, chaplain, was the Prior of St Nicholas' Hospital and Chapel:-

*"A grant by Richard son of William son of Mathew and Beatrice his wife to William son of Mariot of a plot formerly belonging to [?] lord Nicholas Colfox chaplain, late [?] prior of the hospital of St. Nicholas of Wich Malbank, which he [Nicholas] bought from Adam de Berthon, between land of William Colfox and the road to the cemetery in the vill of Wych, rent 1d [penny].*[44] This deed most likely dates to the mid 14th century.

We also know from this deed and other records that Nicholas Colfox, was a knight too, so being both a knight (Lord) and a Chaplain, this means he is likely a Knights Hospitaller (see above and below).

This is likely because he is included as holding land of the Order in Nantwich, under a rental list of the Hospitallers, dating to c1380-1390, see above.[45]

A Nicholas Colfox can be found in deeds dating to: 1339; 1353; 1390/91; 1393; 1404; and 1425.[46] The first deed dating to April 1339 details Nicholas as the son of William Colfox of Wyco Malbano [Nantwich], who as the above grant records, owned a property next to that being transferred.

Nicholas is also detailed as the owner of half a salt work in le Wodestrete (Wood Street in Welsh Row) in Nantwich in 1353.[47]

We also find Nicholas renting properties from Combermere Abbey, because in **'Rentals of Wych Malbanke [Nantwich]'**, dated 1385, recorded in **'The Book of the Abbot of Combermere: 1289 to 1529, Edited by James Hall, The Record Society of Lancashire and Cheshire, Volume 31, 1896, Page 43'**, under High Street, we find *"Nicholas Collfox holds two messuages [properties] and pays yearly, 28 s[hillings]."*

He also has his own Wikipedia page @ https://en.wikipedia.org/wiki/Nicholas_Colfox, which tells us that he was involved in the murder of Thomas of Woodstock, First Duke of Gloucester, Justice of Chester, and hated uncle of King Richard II, in 1397. Whilst others involved in the murder were punished, Nicholas was pardoned sometime after the death of the others, for reasons unknown. However, the reason he may have escaped capital punishment may have been because he had acted on the orders of his friend, and King, Richard II.

He was pardoned sometime after the deposition of King Richard II in 1404, after petitioning King Henry IV to pardon him for the part he held in the murder of Thomas Woodstock. It may also possibly be because he was a Hospitaller, and had also been protected by the Order.

Thomas of Woodstock's murder was made famous by Geoffrey Chaucer's **'Nun's Priest's Tale'**, and William Shakespeare's **'Richard II'** unfinished play.

Earlier in 1393 it is supposed that a rising took place in Cheshire against Thomas of Woodstock, Duke of Gloucester, whilst he was Justice of Chester. He was very much disliked by the county's nobles, never mind the king, but was proclaimed innocent, removed, and another person was appointed by Richard II in his place.[48]

It is believed that there were a number of Colfoxs with the name Nicholas. In **'Early Nantwich Deeds, Allan Murray Wilson, 2010, PP 653'**, we are told that there was a: Nicholas Colfox in the mid 13th century, father of; Nicholas and William Colfox in the late 13th to early 14th century, with William being the father of; Nicholas Colfox (the Elder) in the mid to late 14th century, and believed to have died in 1369/70, with a wife called Matilda, and he was the father of; Nicholas Colfox (the Younger) who lived in the mid to late 14th century too.

This, therefore, means that Nicholas Colfox the Elder was the likely *"chaplain, late [?] prior of the hospital of St. Nicholas of Wich Malbank"*, and his son, Nicholas Colfox the Younger, was most likely linked with the murder of Thomas of Woodstock.

Interestingly too, in **'A History of the Church of Saint Mary, Nantwich: to the Dissolution of The Monasteries, 1536, Francis Blacklay, 1998'**, tells us that he believed Nicholas Colfox was the clerk of Nantwich St Mary's in c1275 to c1285. This may be Nicholas Colfox, brother to William Colfox, who are both included as witnesses in a c1260-90 deed.[49]

* * * * * * *

* * * * * * *

# The Royal Benefactors of Nantwich St Mary's "Hidden in Plain Sight"

Richard II (1367-1400) (reign 1377-1399), spent a great deal of money in Cheshire and Chester, whilst touring the country to drum up support against his Parliament, who denied his raising of funds for the French Wars. He installed his friend and councillor, Robert de Vere, as the Justice of Chester, and created a loyal base of military power in Cheshire. He utilised many Cheshire Archers in his military forces and was popular amongst the folk of Cheshire and their ruling nobles.

The Cheshire Palatinate became known as Richard II's 'inner citadel' of his kingdom, from the supply of knights, archers, and soldiers from the county. Under Richard, it became its own principality, with its ruling nobles rising up the ladder of privilege and position within the kingdom.[50] He is known to have visited Chester at least six times in 1398-9.[51]

King Richard II is also thought to have stayed in Nantwich in 1398, whilst on route to Chester.[52]

His father was also strongly associated with Cheshire, Edward the Black Prince (1330-1376), also known as 'Edward of Woodstock', who had been made the Earl of Chester, by his father the king, in March 1333. This title was conferred upon the young prince, due to the instability of his father's throne, Edward III (1312-1377) (reign 1327-1377), who was having trouble with support from his barons. He also became the Duke of Cornwall (in February 1337), and was the first English Duke. As well as those titles, he was also the Prince of Wales, from May 1343 until his death, as well as being the Prince of Aquitaine and Gascony from 1362.[53] He died in June 1376 and was buried at Canterbury on 29 September.

Edward the Black Prince was much involved in Aquitaine during the Hundred Years' War with France, and its many campaigns. He chose the emblem of the Ostrich feathers, as his heraldic badge, which is now synonymous with the Prince of Wales, or Heir Apparent. During the Battle of Crecy, in 1346, King John of Bohemia, who was blind, and was known as 'John the Blind', was killed, and Edward copied his personal badge, which included the bird's feathers as a heraldic symbol. At the victory of Poitiers in 1356, he fought alongside a number of Cheshire nobles, who were distinguished for their bravery.

He is said to have had at the battle, 101 men-at-arms and 240 archers from Cheshire and North Wales, many having a long tradition of serving the Prince.[54]

Cheshire's famous archers were decisive in the victory at Crecy in 1346, Poitiers in 1356, and Najera in 1367, in the early years of the Hundred Years' War. Every village had shooting butts for the teaching of children of the mighty longbow, and the best were handpicked to serve their nobles and fight for king and country. Living in the northern Marches meant they often got to use and hone their skills in the many skirmishes with the Welsh. Cheshire's archers also fought against the Scots too. They were also the trusted bodyguard of King Richard II, and were often protected from justice for criminal acts including murder, much like Sir Nicholas Colfox was exonerated for his part in the murder of Thomas of Woodstock (see above).

Cheshire nobles who served the Black Prince, we are told by David S. Green in his **'The Military Personnel of Edward the Black Prince, David S. Green, Medieval Prosopography, Volume 21, 2000, Page 141'**, that they included: James Audley; John Delves; John Brunham; David Cradock; and members of the Mascy, Danyers, and Legh families.

He was known as the 'Black Prince' either due to the: colour of his armour; his black shield with three ostrich feathers; or due to his brutal reputation towards the French.

However current consensus believes the nickname to be derived from his black shield with three Ostrich feathers emblazoned, and his matching coloured coat over his armour, rather than anything to do with any brutality against the French. In heraldry, black is a rare colour, so it would have been noticed by the nobility as something unusual, and that is thought why that colour was attached to his name.

In 1353 the Black Prince was accompanied by his loyal noble, Henry of Grosmont, Duke of Lancaster, when trouble erupted at assizes in Chester, which they put down, and took many properties and money. On the way back from seizing a large amount of money from Chester's assizes, along with Henry, the Black Prince passed Vale Royal Abbey near Winsford (not Dieulacres Abbey in Staffordshire as stated in records wrongly), which Edward I had founded (but was not finished), his great grandfather. At this time, the Prince gave a gift of 500 marks out of the vast sum of money he had seized at Chester, so it could be completed. He stayed in the shire for two months, whilst he conducted his business and raised money and further loyalties. He again visited Chester for a short time in 1358.

\* \* \* \* \* \* \*

Edward II (1284-1327) (reign 1307-1327), the Black Prince's grandfather, had much power in Cheshire. Whilst Prince he had been made the Earl of Chester in 1301, by his father Edward I. He was granted the Earldom of Chester, with many of the Palatine's lands across North Wales. He was also the first to hold the Prince of Wales title, which he was invested with, in 1301 at Lincoln.

Edward I (1239-1307) (reign 1272-1307), the Black Prince's great grandfather, famously conquered and militarised Wales, amongst many other exploits, including campaigns against the Scots and the French.

King Edward I founded Vale Royal Abbey, near Winsford, to the north of Nantwich, in c1270 as a house of the Cistercians (like Combermere Abbey, and its daughter house, Whalley Abbey in Lancashire was). It is believed that the legend of the Abbey's founding came about after Edward I, then Prince, was nearly shipwrecked during crossing the Channel in the 1260s. After that act of God, he had vowed to build a House of God, to praise the Virgin Mary, whom he had pleaded with in prayer, to spare his life, which immediately calmed the storm after his supposition to her. However other researchers now believe that the foundation charter, dating to August 1270, means the abbey had a Crusader connection, because he left for the Holy Land in 1270, and likely dedicated the church to St Mary, when pleading for her protection whilst on Crusade.

Interestingly, Edward is said to have donated a relic of the True Cross to the Abbey, after his Crusade in the Holy Land. Could this be linked with the Guild or Brethren of the Holy Cross, see later?

\* \* \* \* \* \* \*

Also, Sir William Mainwaring of Baddiley and Peover, whose medieval alabaster effigy still exists in the nearby Church of St Mary's at Acton, was believed to have given *"a piece of the holy cross set in wax"* to the church, on his death in 1399.[55] He was a known Crusader, and must have bought the relic back from the Holy Land.

Another local knight, this time Sir Hugh de Calveley (c1315-94), whose alabaster effigy still exists at St Boniface's Church at Bunbury, was involved in the Hundred Years' War in France. He also served in Spain. He had also been the Seneschal of the port city of Calais, Admiral of the English Fleet, as well as the Governor of the Channel Islands. From French war booty, he paid for the rebuilding of Bunbury Church's chancel and for the building of an attached chantry chapel for eleven priests. He established the Church as a collegiate church, in the 1380s. He had also served under the Black Prince and was a friend of him.

\* \* \* \* \* \* \*

Vale Royal Abbey took some time to complete, due to the Welsh Wars, funds were short, never mind the effects of the Black Death, and work faltered. As above the Black Prince, gave funds for work to resume, and the work progressed in the late 14th century, when his son Richard II was on the throne, but the abbey was reduced in size, due to excessive costs.

Vale Royal was dedicated to St Mary the Virgin, St Nicholas, and St Nicasius, which proves interesting for St Mary's Church of Nantwich, because it was believed to be dedicated to the Blessed [St] Mary and St Nicholas, and the brass Eagle lectern, carries that inscription. The Kingsley Chapel in the South Transept is also known as the Chapel of St Nicholas, and has been known under that dedication since 1922, according to a brass plaque, on the southern wall. This dedication may have been reinstated from what the older two-thirds of the South Transept may have already been dedicated to, when six chantry chapels existed in the church, as revealed in 1548, during the Dissolution. And as we know the Chapel and Hospital which gave its name to Hospital Street, was dedicated to St Nicholas.

In the North Transept, St George's Chapel still exists to the southern two-thirds (although it is thought it was originally further west, to the north-east part of the Nave), whilst the timber screen, with original tall stone arch, which separates the northern third, was originally the Lady Chapel or Chapel of Our Lady, dedicated like the whole church, to the Blessed Virgin Mary.

There was also another Chantry Chapel with an altar we know existed in the Church, which was the chantry of St James.

There must have also been a chantry for the 'Guild of the Holy Cross', presumably dedicated to the Cross.

The Priest's Vestry or the Old Treasury, to the north-east of the Chancel, was sometimes known as 'The Old Crypt' and it has a piscina (a stone bowl in a stone recess for the priest to wash his hands and the equipment of the rituals of mass); like those found in the Lady Chapel, St George's Chapel, St Nicholas's (or the Kingsley) Chapel, and by the High Altar, and indicates that this part of the church, was also once a Chantry Chapel. This may indicate that this was the original resting place of Sir David Cradock, and his tomb, being next to the Sanctuary and High Altar. It is of two storeys, and there was once a spiral staircase to its north-west corner. It also has aumbry cupboards, for books and church plate, and a wafer-bread oven with a flue.

\* \* \* \* \* \* \*

Vale Royal Abbey's time-consuming and stop-start construction is reminiscent of Nantwich St Mary's. Like Vale Royal, it took a long time with periods of stagnation, and the interruptions of the Black Death, to complete.

The current St Mary's Church was begun in around 1340, although part of the church structure which existed to the earlier church on the site, remained, i.e. the smaller Red Sandstone blocks to the lower half of the North Aisle. Parts of the foundations of the North Transept and the Crossing, the plan of the Chancel, and before Sir George Gilbert Scott's mid Victorian renovation, replaced the earlier West front, date or dated to the 13$^{th}$ century.

The earlier church may have been built by the Abbey of Combermere, and an earlier benefactor, Lord Robert Burnell, Bishop of Bath and Wells and Lord Chancellor of England. His relations, John Riparriis and Hugh Plissitis, conceded their rights of the Barony of Wych Malbank and the Advowson (right to appoint a priest) of the Church of Wych Malbank to Robert.[56]

According to **'The Quire and Misericords of St Mary's Parish Church, Nantwich, Cheshire, by Percy Newton Corry, 1974'**, King Edward I in a deed dated 19 May 1283: *"Granted to the venerable father Robert, Bishop of Bath and Wells that he and his heirs for ever shall have a fair at His Manor of Wych Malbank, in the county of Chester every year for three days duration"*. As Lord Chancellor of England, Bishop Robert would have been an intimate friend of Edward I.

This fits nicely with Edward I's foundation charter of the nearby Vale Royal Abbey, also a Cistercian Monastery, dedicated to the Virgin, like Combermere, in August 1270, as explained above.

Interestingly, R. E. Pritchard, in his **'St Mary's, Nantwich: A Pitkin Guide, 1991'**, tells us that *"in 1277 Vale Royal Abbey was begun by Robert Burnell, Chancellor of England and Bishop of Bath and Wells [presumably on Edward I's behalf], [and] who was probably responsible in the 1280s for beginning on the site of St Mary's [Nantwich] a church with similar cruciform plan and area as this one. That may have been completed, and little survives."*

R. E. Pritchard also tells us that the current church *"in the 1340s rebuilding in the flowing curvilinear Decorated style begun by Yorkshire masons (associated with York and Beverley Ministers, and the cruciform church at Partington). This work in turn was interrupted, probably by the Black Death plagues between 1349 and 1369"*. And that by (either the 1370s or the) late 1380s *"building in the new, stiffer Perpendicular style was then carried out by master masons associated with Lichfield and Gloucester cathedrals and familiar with recent East Anglian work (notably the octagonal towers of Ely and nearby Sutton)"*.

We know that St Mary's Church began in the Gothic Style known as 'Decorated', some windows were or still are in this style, whilst others are later, or replaced or repaired during renovations. Part of the Tower's lower eastern construction and stonework is also of an earlier mid 14$^{th}$ century date, as well as parts of the nave, choir, and chancel, to the majority of the body of the Cruciform church. Again like Vale Royal, the Black Death took its toll, and this may be shown in the change of design, once work restarted, with the pillar to the junction of the North Aisle and North Transept, finishing abruptly only part of its intended height. This may be indicative of a redesign by the new team of later masons.[57 & 58] However, this pillar is definitely later than the North Aisle wall because you can see how the stone blocks and mortar courses to its immediate west, have been made to fit. This evidence may infer it was actually installed after the Black Death period, and it had an entirely different function and meaning.

By the 1370s work continued, and at pace, but in the later 'Perpendicular' Gothic style, and by the final stages of the 14$^{th}$ century, the building was practically finished, with just a few parts dating to the early years of the 15$^{th}$ century.

This stop-start nature of the construction during the 14$^{th}$ century is reflected in the differences in design, especially the majority of the Crossing and the Chancel to the rest of the Church.

It is believed that St Mary's was completed in the early years of the 15$^{th}$ century because in 1405 the Bishop of Lichfield licenced the Chapel [Church] of Nantwich to celebrate divine service.

Other parts date to: the mid to late 15$^{th}$ century, such as: the third southern end of the South Transept, once known as the Kingsley Chapel, but now as St Nicholas' Chapel; the South Porch; or the early 16$^{th}$ century; and the Clerestory above the Nave, to the late 16$^{th}$ / early 17$^{th}$ century.

\* \* \* \* \* \* \*

Sadly, Black Prince Edward predeceased his father, by a year, aged 45, so his son Richard II ascended to the throne. The Black Prince had supported the nobility of Cheshire, and Richard II his son also supported them. Richard visited often in the late 1390s and stayed at Chester Castle. It is likely that he gave money towards the building of St Mary's Church in Nantwich, as well as the Black Prince, over the mid to late 14th century. Vale Royal Abbey had royal money expended upon it, as well as presumably countless others. It is also possible that Nicholas Colfox, as well as other local Nantwich nobility, supported the building of the magnificent edifice.

Combermere Abbey held the Chapel of Wych Malbank [Nantwich], according to historic deeds dating to 1277, when the Dean and Chapter of Lichfield confirmed their church and chapel holdings.

We also know that Combermere Abbey during the reign of Edward III, was under royal protection, but not in custody, when it defended its rights to Acton, Sandon, and Alstonfield churches, in 1383.[59]

Previously in 1354, Edward the Black Prince, Edward III's eldest son, restored the lease of Wincle Grange to the Abbey to farm.[60]

In 1388 Robert, the Abbot of Combermere was made the 'Justice in Eyre' (a travelling magistrate presiding over a (hundred) court, bringing justice for the King's Law to an area they were responsible for) for Nantwich and Middlewich.[61]

We know from a historic deed dated 9 May 1277, that the Dean and Chapter of Lichfield confirmed that Combermere Abbey held: the churches of Acton [by Nantwich], Sandon [Staffordshire], and Alstonefield [Staffordshire]; the chapels of Wych Malbank [Nantwich], Wrenbury, [Church] Minshull, and Derefold [Dorfold].[62]

* * * * * * *

A stone arch keystone and vault springer under and to the Tower and North Transept Arch certainly is reminiscent of Edward III, and reminiscent of known portraits of him.

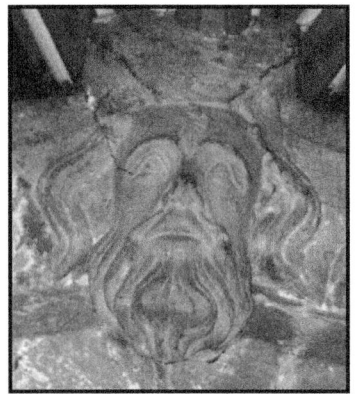 

*Is this Carved Stone Corbel Keystone under the Tower's North Arch of St Mary's Church, Nantwich, a Representation of King Edward III? (Left) & King Edward III's Bronze Effigy Head in Westminster Abbey (Right)*
Right Image Source (Public Domain):https://en.wikipedia.org/wiki/ Edward_III_of_England#/media/File:Edward-III-king-England.jpg

The other tower arch keystones and vault springers depict: possibly a bearded Warrior with a Helmet (to the East); a Queen with a square-shaped headdress (to the South); and an owl (which in the Middle Ages was a symbol of death and tombs, and as a harbinger of doom, because it was thought as an ill omen, with it being a night creature) (to the West).

These keystones are all that is left of the original stone vaulted ribs, which would have sprung from these four corbels, and the corner pillar capitals (if the vault ever existed, unlike the never completed vaulted ceiling of the Lady Chapel in the North Transept). The ceiling was most likely replaced in: 1609, when "the steeple' (a term then commonly used instead of 'tower') called for attention, and besides re-roofing *"two floors were made new"*;[63] and again by the extensive restoration by the Victorian architect Sir George Gilbert Scott in c1855-61, as the slightly higher painted timber vault ribs reveal.[64]

We know that the tower's stone vaulted ceiling no longer existed by the time of Sir George Gilbert Scott's Restoration, because only the vault springers remained in a drawing of the Crossing of St Mary's Church, titled **'Inside View of Part of the Chancel, &c. of**

***Nantwich Church, Cheshire: Taken from the South Transept, Published by T. Cadell & W. Davies, May, 1. 1809'***, which appeared on page 440 of ***'Magna Britannia; Being a Concise Topographical Account of the Several Counties of Great Britain, Volume II: Cambridgeshire and Cheshire, Daniel and Samuel Lysons, 1810'***, see the next page for that engraved drawing.

*Inside View of Part of the Chancel, &c. of
Nantwich Church, Cheshire: Taken from the South Transept,
Published by T. Cadell & W. Davies, May, 1. 1809*

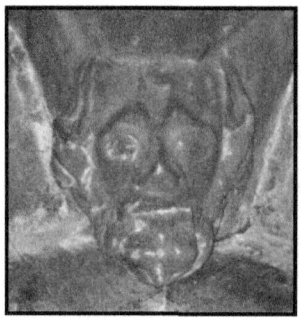  

*The Other Three Corbels to the East, South, and West, of St Mary's Tower Arches*

If the northern tower corbel is in fact Edward III, then it is likely the others are: his wife, Queen Philippa of Hainault, opposite in the South (above middle); and if a helmeted warrior (with bascinet helmet), his son Edward the Black Prince to the East (above left); with an Owl representing that he had died whilst his father lived, opposite him in the West (above right).

The Owl being in the West is also representative of the Sun setting upon the Prince's short life. As well as its added symbolism of gazing down upon the world, keeping a watchful and guarding eye, and its association with wisdom. It is also a symbol of rebirth and transformation, hence the Prince then and now being, in the life up above.

We are told in **'Interpreting Medieval Corbel Sculpture, Richard Halsey, Historic Churches, 2015'**, that *"portraits can be more confidently identified as such when a man and woman face each other or face down into the congregation from the corbels adjacent to the tower or rood loft, suggesting they are the patrons."* This, therefore tells us that the portrait corbels here, which are likely 14$^{th}$ century Royals, are most likely the benefactors or patrons of Nantwich St Mary's.

This certainly seems very likely, when we look at a drawing of the effigies of Edward III and Queen Philippa, at Westminster, and compare their forms under Nantwich's Octagonal Tower, see next page.

**Effigies of Edward III. and Queen Philippa;
from their tombs in Westminster Abbey**
Source (Public Domain):
https://en.wikipedia.org/wiki/Philippa_of_Hainault#/media/File:EDuard_Filpa.jpg

We also see that Queen Philippa is wearing on her effigy, a very similar headdress like a flat hood with perpendicular sides, like she is depicted with at Nantwich. This headdress is an elaborate reticulated head-dress (where the hair was encased on either side of the head in bags made of gold or silver thread).

Due to much of the later stages of St Mary's Church dating to the 1370s to c1400, it is very likely that Richard II, finished off what may have begun, under his grandfather, King Edward III's reign, and under the jurisdiction of his father, Edward the Black Prince, and had these high up keystone corbels carved as the heads of his immediate ancestors. Namely, his father the Black Prince, who would have been king if he hadn't have died young, and his grandparents and predecessor, Edward III, and his wife, Queen Philippa. What better way to celebrate your ancestry and noble birth, than set your loved ones in stone, for future posterity, or even for time immemorial?

A further proof that Edward III is depicted at the apex of the Northern Arch of the Crossing, which is directly in front of the North Transept, is that St George's Chapel is located here. Edward III founded the Order of the Garter, with St George as its patron. As well as that St George was made: the patron saint of England; the saintly protector of the royal family; and the Cross of St George became the emblem of England; during Edward III's reign.

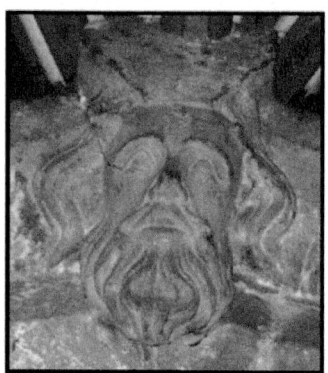 

***Comparison of the Two Royal? Portraits in Stone at St Mary's Crossing, compared to their Westminster Abbey effigies***

Richard II is also thought to have been a Royal Patron of building works to: the Crossing of the Abbey of St Werburgh [Chester Cathedral], which at the same time the late 14th century choir stalls were created; as well as at St John's Church in Chester, when the refounding of the fraternity of St Anne in 1393 took place.[65]

According to **'Master Masons of the Diocese of Lichfield: A Study in 14th Century Architecture at the Time of the Black Death, JM Maddison, Transactions of the Lancashire and Cheshire Antiquarian Society, Volume 85, 1988 (with Notes), Page 12'**, *"the elevation of the choir of Lichfield provides a most important and immediate diocesan precedent, but the proportions at Chester [Cathedral] are much more closely related to the choirs of Selby and Howden, both of which allow a generous area of wall between the clerestory windows, a feature which the more sophisticated work at Lichfield eliminates by the use of larger windows and by running the various jambs and vault shafts together. If Phase Three may be assigned to the late 1340s, it is quite conceivable that the arcades of Phase Four are connected with* **the letters of protection issued by the Black Prince in 1354 for 'twelve of the masons, carpenters and other workmen continually employed by the abbot and convent on the works of the church.' With subtly altered details, this building campaign seems to continue into the south aisle of the nave, and it is possible that further letters of protection issued by the Prince on 1st October 1363 for the abbot of Chester's masons may have been in part connected with this continuing project.**"

This, therefore, gives evidence that not only Richard II was involved, but also the Black Prince was also, with phases of construction of St Werburgh's Abbey [Chester Cathedral] in the mid to late 14th century.

The same publication also tells us on **'Page 18'**, that in 1354 when work was still going on at Chester, that: *"In the same year it appears that the chancel of Warrington, Cheshire, was in hand, and stylistic analogies imply that the chancel of Malpas, Cheshire (later rebuilt), was being constructed at the same time. Windows similar in character to those at Warrington are to be found widely scattered, for example at Albrighton, Salop, and at Cossal and Penkridge, Staffordshire. In 1356 the now vanished bell tower of*

*Whalley Abbey [Combermere's Sister House] in Lancashire was rising, as we know from the recorded death from a falling stone of brother Ralph of Pontefract, but* **the most important work of this decade was undoubtedly the new east end of Vale Royal Abbey, a project which had been contemplated since 1353 when the Black Prince made a grant of 500 marks towards the completion of the church. In 1358 he made a further grant of the same amount, and in June of the following year a contract was drawn up between the abbot and convent and Master William de Helpeston** *who, like Henry de Snelleston the Prince's mason, was already actively involved in the maintenance of the royal castles in Cheshire and North Wales. The document is one of the first really detailed building contracts in English medieval architecture, and Knoop and Jones believed that the introduction of the contract system was speeded up by the effects of the Black Death on the availability and cost of labour. It is equally significant that work could not begin until 1358, for the abbot wrote to the prince in February 1354 to explain that it had not been possible to obtain sufficient masons and carpenters to begin the work."*

Also on **'Pages 59-60'** we find that: *"In the late 14th century Cheshire experienced a resurgence of royal interest of which the most significant known architectural consequence was the rebuilding, with the agreement of Richard II, of the nave of Vale Royal Abbey. William Wynford, who built the later parts of the nave of Winchester, was a royal mason and, therefore, a colleague of the king's masons who were continually drawn to Chester and North Wales to work on the king's castles, so there would have been no impediment to the rapid transfer of ideas and to enrichment of the Perpendicular master's repertory with some of the latest architectural devices."*

According to **'Rural Economy and Society in the Duchy of Cornwall, 1300-1500, John Hatcher, 2008, & The Military Personnel of Edward the Black Prince, David S. Green, Medieval Prosopography, Volume 21, 2000, Pages 133-152'**, Edward the Black Prince, and his *"estates were often governed with a degree of benevolence that far exceeded the feudal obligations of a lord to his tenants, and with a spirit of charity pitifully wanting in the administration of many ecclesiastic estates at this time"*. This certainly adds to the evidence of him, and likely his father, and his son, being involved with the building or extending of many religious buildings in the areas they had held interests in, compared to the poor funding from the Church authorities.

The Black Prince's charity and benevolence is also shown in **'The Ledger Book of the Vale Royal Abbey, edited by John Brownbill, Manchester Record Society, 1914'**, where we are told under Folio 97, that *"the abbot and convent of Vale Royal, have received from the lord, our Lord Edward [the Black Prince], son of the illustrious King of England [Edward III], Prince of Aquitaine and of Wales, Duke of Cornwall and Earl of Chester, by the hands of Master John de Brunham, chamberlain of Chester, one cask of red wine of Gascony from the prise of the same lord at Chester, granted to us of old time for celebrating divine service in our abbey of Vale Royal"*. Other entries in the Ledger, also state that casks of Gascony red wine were often gifted to the thankful Abbey under the orders of the Black Prince, and his Chester chamberlain.

The Prince was also involved in the appropriation of St Padarn's Church of Llanbadarn Fawr (near Aberystwyth in Ceredigion), to the abbey, in 1359/60. Vale Royal held the church until 1538.

In Cheshire, the Prince had over £1,500 paid to him in annuities.[66]

In **'The Black Prince, H. J. Hewitt, Cheshire Round, Volume 1, No. 10, Summer 1969, Page 324'**, we are told that *"the aggregate amount derived from the earldom [of Cheshire] in the early years of the [14$^{th}$] century had been about £1,500 to £1,900 and had subsequently fallen. In 1353-4, it reached £3,928 and there were several more years of very high revenue as the instalments of the fines were being paid."*

\* \* \* \* \* \* \*

I wonder if Nikolaus Pevsner and Edward Hubbard in their architectural guide, **'The Buildings of England: Cheshire, 1986, Pages 285-287'**, realised when they remarked that St Mary's Nantwich: *"then, as one looks up, one sees at once the crowning motif of the church, the octagonal crossing tower"*; that it certainly was, inside, at each of the four North, South, East, and West

Tower Arches, and their arch keystones and vault springers; figurative of their 14$^{th}$ century Royal Patrons?

It is also a great place for the souls of the Royal Benefactors and Patrons to view all who worship in their church, the centre of the town, from its completion to the modern day, and onwards, from up on high, below the Tower, the heart of the Cruciform Church. It thus was meant to remind all, of their charity to the people of Nantwich, albeit lost until now to the mists of time, yet 'hidden in plain sight', all along.

They stare out from the Crossing, between the lay folk of the Nave, the nobility, and the original chantry chapels of the North and South Transepts, and the Priest-only area of the Chancel and Sanctuary.

Why else would they be depicted by master masons' skill, if not the main benefactors of this mainly mid to late 14$^{th}$ century monument, often coined the 'Cathedral of South Cheshire'? Who else but royalty would have had the weighty purse to spend on such a magnificent and extensive House of God?

Of course, other benefactors would have added to the pot of funds, some of which we visited above, and some below, such as: Sir David Cradock, Knight, thought to be the 14$^{th}$ century church's founder (below); the Abbot and Monks of Combermere Abbey; the Guild or Brethren of the Holy Cross (below); Sir Nicholas Colfox, Knight (above); the Praers; John Kingsley Esquire; and possibly: Sir William Mainwaring of Acton; Sir John Griffin; Sir Alan Cheyne; the Knights Hospitaller (above); the Fouleshursts; the Lord Lovells; as well as the town's folk themselves; as well as others yet to be fully determined.

Also if we remember that nearly all churches before the Reformation, had a rood screen, i.e. a large ornately carved wooden screen with Christ impaled upon the Crucifix above, at the entrance to the Chancel, or in this case between the Crossing and the Chancel, then: here we have Edward III, his Queen Philippa, and their son, Edward the Black Prince, staring down from above the Son of God. How much more lofty can a Royal or Royals be in an earthly house of God?

\* \* \* \* \* \* \*

A boss to the ceiling of the Chancel of the Church, depicting the Conception, links with Combermere Abbey and is an exact copy of the Abbot's seal, which was used to authorise their documents.[67]

\* \* \* \* \* \* \*

It is also revealed in **'A History of the Church of Saint Mary, Nantwich: to the Dissolution of The Monasteries, 1536, Francis Blacklay, 1998',** that one of the misericords in the Choir of St Mary's, on the south side, and not far from the west end, according to Percy Newton Corry, consist of [King Richard in the middle], with *"the one on the left is Hugh Herland, King Richard's Master Carpenter, and probably the one on the right is that of the King's Master Mason, Henry Yevele. Together they were responsible for Richard's re-roofing [of] Westminster Hall in the glorious single span which we see to-day; also for the chancel of Saint Mary's Nantwich. In complete contrast is the roughly carved head of a king which might well have been the work of a clumsy and inexperienced apprentice. The sardonic censorious smile of the face on the left tells all as it registers the discomfort of Henry IV on receiving a blast of pulse fed monkish flatus straight in the face. Repaired damage shows an attempt to remove the seat. Henry IV did not remain ignorant. In the general amnesty that had eventually to be granted to the Cheshire rebels, the Vicar of Nantwich was excluded; the Vicar of Acton was the only other exclusion but that was only to mask the real reason".*

Henry Yevele according to **'Henry Yevele: The Life of an English Architect, John H. Harvey, 1946, Pages 54-68'**, and his Wikipedia page (https://en.wikipedia.org/wiki/Henry_Yevele), worked on many domestic, civil, military, and ecclesiastical buildings, as well as funerary monuments, as a master mason. Those which he was responsible for and are relevant to this study were: part of the Black Prince's Kennington Manor (London) [destroyed]; works at the Tower of London, including the Bloody Tower; the Abbot's House (later Deanery) and College Hall (Westminster); Westminster Abbey Nave and West Cloister; the Clock Tower to the Palace of Westminster [destroyed]; St Thomas' Chapel on London Bridge [destroyed]; the high altar screen to Durham Cathedral (North East England); the East and South walks of the Cloister of St Albans Abbey (Hertfordshire); the South Transept facade of Old St Paul's Cathedral (London) [destroyed]; a new South Aisle and Porch at St Dunstan's in the East (London) [destroyed]; Canterbury Cathedral Nave and South Cloister (Kent); Westminster Hall (Houses of Parliament, Westminster); Edward III's and Queen Philippa's Tomb, and Richard II's Tomb, both at Westminster Abbey; the Black Prince's Tomb at Canterbury Cathedral; John of Gaunt's Tomb in Old St Paul's Cathedral; Cardinal Simon Langham's Tomb in Westminster Abbey; and Archbishop Simon Sudbury's Tomb in Canterbury Cathedral.

Henry Yevele also presided over and had influenced many mid to late 14$^{th}$ century building projects other than those listed above, around the country, some of which cannot be fully verified.

It is also interesting to note that Richard II's Master Mason, Henry, whose surname was Yevele, is believed to be derived from the village of Ye[a]veley in Derbyshire. This is where the Knights Hospitaller Cheshire Estates, including what they held in Nantwich, and its surrounding area, were controlled and administered from. At Yeaveley, the Order had a commandery or preceptory, which was like a large monastic grange, with its own chapel or church, and manor house. Please see above. The family of Yeaveley, from which Henry is believed to have descended, dates back in historical records to the 12$^{th}$ century.

John Harvey in **'English Medieval Architects: A Biographical Dictionary down to 1550, 1954'**, tells us that Henry Yevele was thought to have lived from circa 1320 to 1400, and was buried at the church of St Magnus the Martyr, near London Bridge; and Hugh Herland, the King's Chief Carpenter, lived from circa 1330-1405[or 1411]. According to Wikipedia (https:// en.Wikipedia.org/wiki/Hugh_Herland), Hugh also worked on Westminster Palace, the Tower of London, and the Tombs of Edward III and Queen Philippa.

It is also stated in the above source, that Master Mason Yevele was *"the greatest of English architects"* and that he *"developed fully the intrinsically English style which we call perpendicular"*. We are also told that he was a *"very remarkable and busy man [who] worked for the Black Prince and also as the King's 'deviser of masonry' ('deviser' loosely means 'designer'), [in 1362]"*, and that *"he worked on both castles and bridges"*.

Henry Yevele was also termed 'director of works' in documents of 1365 and 1378.[68]

Whether or not Master Yevele was involved in the building, coordinating, overseeing or delegating, of the construction of any part of St Mary's Church in Nantwich, cannot be fully proven. Although we now know that Richard II, and his father and grandfather, were likely royal benefactors.

In support of Henry Yevele being involved with Nantwich, Canterbury Cathedral's lierne vaulted nave, which dates from 1391 to 1405, was undertaken by royal *"court masons"* and is said to be *"of the Nantwich type"*, and that they *"are remarkably alike"*, as well as Canterbury's cloisters, dating to 1397 [now believed to date to the early 15th century], are *"also a parallel phenomenon"*, detailed in **'Master Masons of the Diocese of Lichfield: A Study in 14th Century Architecture at the Time of the Black Death, JM Maddison, Transactions of the Lancashire and Cheshire Antiquarian Society, Volume 85, 1988 (with Notes), Page 36'**. Although also detailed, Nantwich's vault is somewhat slightly earlier, but in further support, is less complex than Canterbury's.

It is also interesting to note that Edward the Black Prince, held Canterbury Cathedral close to his heart, and had been a great benefactor to it. He had a chantry chapel created in its crypt where he hoped to be buried. He was instead buried in its Trinity Chapel near to St Thomas Becket's shrine, with a magnificent Purbeck marble chest tomb, embellished with enamelled shields and gilding, and with a life-size effigy of Edward, made of gilded copper alloy, covered in the English and French royal coat of arms. That coat of arms was created for his family's wish to be both Kings of England and France, which the Hundred Years' War was all about. The tomb also depicts his Prince of Wales coat of arms, those of three Ostrich's feathers; he had taken from the heraldry of John the Blind, who fell at the Prince's victory at Crecy in 1346.

This, therefore, gives another link between Canterbury and Nantwich, and their vaulted ceilings, and depictions of Edward, the

Black Prince, whether in stone or copper; and possibly the Royal Master Mason, Henry Yevele, who is also thought to have created his stone chest tomb, beneath his effigy.

The Master Mason of St Mary's Church may be depicted in carved stone on the north-western column of the Crossing, to the immediate bottom right of the Green Man carving, staring northward. Henry Yevele is believed to be depicted, albeit now rather worn, at Westminster Abbey's Cloisters, where he is carved nearby to King Edward III and his wife Queen Philippa, as well as the Black Prince. Is this further evidence of Nantwich's Royal Patronage, and the King's Master Mason, again appearing together with the Royals?

Also, at Ely Cathedral in Cambridgeshire two stone carvings presumably of Edward III and Queen Philippa appear opposite each other in the Crossing, beneath the octagonal lantern (see links: http://www.greenend.org.uk/rjk/gallery/photos/2006/0719?display=IMG_2028.JPG & http://www.greenend.org.uk/rjk/gallery_/photos/2006/07-19?display=_IMG_2030.JPG#IMG_2030.JPG). These, like Nantwich's, are beneath the Crossing, however, they do not match Henry Yevele's portraits of the royal couple on their Westminster Abbey tomb effigies, whereas, Nantwich's likely carvings of them do.

The misericords remaining from the once standing Hospital of St Katherine by the Tower, in London, also feature Edward III and Queen Philippa, but in wood (see link: https://spitalfieldslife.com/2016/09/22/misericords-at-st-katharines-chapel/). These, are similar to their effigies at Westminster, but are both crowned. Edward III has his long hair, but swept back around the timber misericord elbow, as well as his large moustache and beard. Queen Philippa does have her hair squarely held with gold wire to each side of her head. So therefore, these are in a similar vein to Nantwich's, albeit with crowns and in wood.

St Katherine's by the Tower's c1360 misericords also have a carving of a Master Mason with his masonic flat round cap. This may be Henry Yevele, with his trademark long curly hair. The portrait also shows a strong nose, prominent cheek bones, a moustache but not under the nose, and beard. A Cheshire or Lion Mask, with its tongue protruding also appears at St Katherine's.

Henry Yevele is also thought to appear in stone at Canterbury Cathedral. One in the east walk of the Cloisters, and another in the North Transept St Andrew's Chapel. These two possible depictions show: in the former, an old man with closed eyes, signifying he was dead by the carving's creation, with curly hair, a moustache each side of the nose, and a beard; whilst the latter, shows a younger gentleman, again with curling hair, but a smaller goatee beard, and usual moustache.

**Henry Yevele's Presumed Portraits at Canterbury Cathedral
(Left) St Andrew's Chapel; (Right) Cloisters**

Source and Copyright:
CHAS (Canterbury Historical and Archaeological Society) Website
(https://www. canterbury-archaeology.org.uk/henry-yevele-c-1320-1400)

Nantwich's probable Master Mason does have elaborate curling hair, a moustache, strong cheek bones, and a good nose, and is similar to the others thought to be Yevele, but not enough to definitely prove that all these carvings are of the same man.

\* \* \* \* \* \* \*

The outstanding 69 stone bosses to St Mary's Chancel Lierne Vault are of a high order of medieval sculpture. Their exquisite detail is rather indicative that they were created by the skill of an excellent master mason, and most likely, a royal craftsman.

The form of the likely royal patrons carved below the tower, the adjacent green man, and the likeness of the master mason next to him, are also of a high order of carving, and indicative of a highly skilled master mason.

* * * * * * *

Richard II commissioned both: his father's tomb, the Black Prince (believed to have been created in the mid to late 1380s, and unique at the time with the effigy being made from cast gilded copper alloy); but also Edward III's, his grandfather, with a bearded bronze effigy on a chest tomb at Westminster Abbey. Again like at Nantwich's St Mary's Church, all three are likely distinguished together in their shared patronage.

*Thought to be King Richard II (Centre), his Master Carpenter (Left), and his Master Mason (Right) (with a Masonic Round Cap), on a Misericord Seat in Nantwich St Mary's Choir (5th from the East and on the South Side)*

*The Two Cheshire Lions or Masks, Above the Misericord*

Also above this misericord supposedly depicting King Richard II and his Master Carpenter and Master Mason, are two 'Cheshire Lions' or masks. These types of lion are synonymous with Cheshire, and often appear in its churches carved stone, stained glass, carved wood, and floor tiles. Two examples appear in the North Transept St George's Chapel's East Windows.

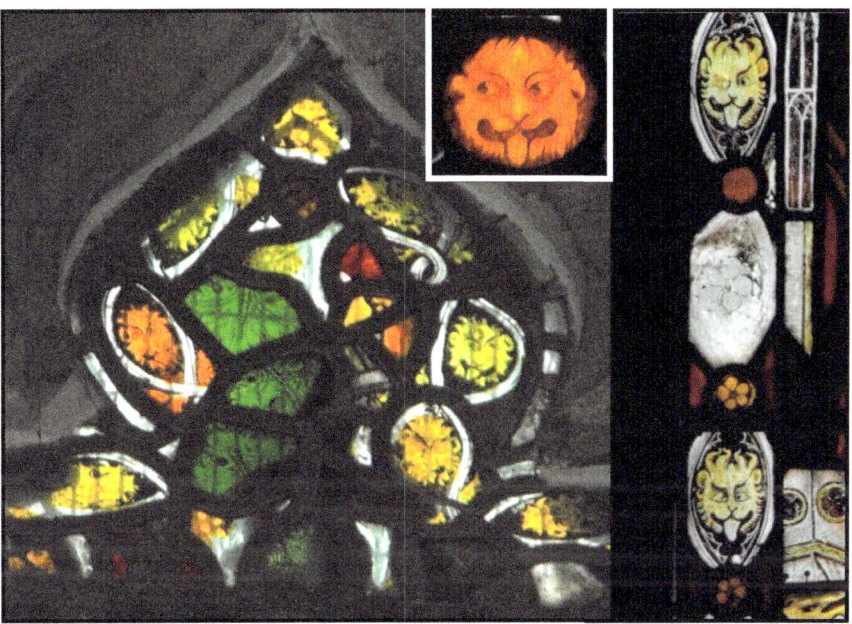

*The re-used Medieval Cheshire Lion Masks to the South-West Window in the Chancel (Left), and South-East Window in St George's Chapel, North Transept (Top Centre), of St Mary's Church, Nantwich; and the re-used Medieval Cheshire Lion Masks to the Window at St John's Church, Keele (Right)*

They are often used by the Chester glaziers in stained glass, and a collection of six lions' heads have also been gathered together in the south-west chancel clerestory of Nantwich St Mary's (see above). They also appear in Keele's Templar Window in the Tower of St John the Baptist's Church in North Staffordshire (also see above).[69]

  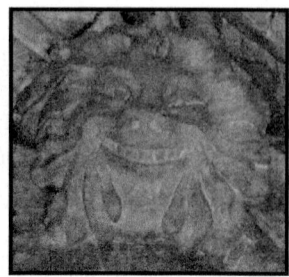

*Cheshire Lions to the West of the Chancel Vault*

There are also three Cheshire Lions as carved vault roof bosses, at the west end of the Chancel, where it meets the Crossing and its Tower. This is rather fitting because the vault corbel and keystone to the east arch of the Crossing, behind these three Cheshire Lions, likely represents the Black Prince.

Numerous examples also appear in stone on the exterior cornice of Nantwich St Mary's 14$^{th}$ century Chancel.

These Cheshire Lions also appear at Chester Cathedral in the carved wood choir misericords, as well as on Victorian (possibly copying earlier medieval) floor tiles.

*Two of the many Cheshire Lion Masks to the exterior of Nantwich St Mary's Chancel*

Do these lions show the link of these royals, King Richard II, his father, grandfather, and grandmother, as well as his master craftsmen, with Cheshire, as we have found above?

***The Cheshire Lion Masks on Edward the Black Prince's Effigy's Sword Belt or Girdle, at Canterbury Cathedral***

**(Reproduced with permission from Dr Jessica Barker, FSA, Senior Lecturer in Medieval Art, The Courtauld Gallery)**

(Source: ''Fully armed in plate of war': making the effigy of the Black Prince, Jessica Barker, Graeme McArthur and Emily Pegues, The Burlington Magazine, Issue 163, November 2021, Pages 997-1009')

The Cheshire Lions or Lion Masks, also appear on Edward the Black Prince's Effigy at Canterbury Cathedral, which was created by his son, Richard II, as we discussed above. On his effigy's sword belt or girdle, we find enamelled champlevé, with the [Cheshire] lion masks in gold foil, surrounded by royal blue enamel.

\* \* \* \* \* \* \*

Another similar misericord appears in the Quire [Choir] at St Werburgh's Cathedral in Chester. These misericords are similar to Nantwich's, and date from the late 14th century, and are believed to be by the School of Hugh Herland. One depicts a bearded and crowned king, with two people in profile supporting him. This misericord is the last one towards the east on the south side of the Quire stalls.

*The Bearded and Crowned King with Two Supporters Eitherside, on a Misericord Seat, at Chester St Werburgh's Cathedral*

*The Cheshire Lions Misericord Seat to the immediate right of the above misericord, at Chester St Werburgh's Cathedral*

\* \* \* \* \* \* \*

The richness of the Choir Stalls and Misericords of St Mary's Nantwich, and their national importance is shown in the **'Misericords of North West England: Their Nature and Significance, John Dickinson, 2008, Pages 39-40'**, where we are told that *"built at the same time as the misericords, the stalls are "of a complexity unsurpassed in English medieval woodcarving." They are an example of tabernacled stalls, "English carvers, greatest triumphs." As well as "[these] accomplishments, to many eyes, reach the pinnacle of craftsmanship. As Francis Bond observes: while the design "of [the Choir Stalls of] Chester [Cathedral] is reminiscent of early fourteenth century work, that of*

*Nantwich is well advanced toward normal fifteenth century design. It is also much richer."* We are also told that *"Nantwich became the standard bearer for stallwork; a fact evidenced when the carvers in Manchester came to create their own work 120 years later. Their ambition was "to surpass" that from Nantwich, but they could not, and ended up simply copying much of the work."*

John Dickinson in the same publication, also adds that Nantwich St Mary's Stone Pulpit is also of national importance, *"the stone masons equalled the work of the wood carvers. The stone pulpit in Nantwich is from the same period as the choir stalls, and with its "slender stalk-like pedestal", its carvings flow from the pulpit into the chancel screen in a delightful manner that has been described as "one of the best examples of ancient stone pulpits in the country." Similarly, the octagonal crossing tower, ... , is a rare and beautiful example of the type."*

This just adds even more weight that Nantwich St Mary's had Royal Patrons, and their Craftsmen, were involved with its construction and design.

\* \* \* \* \* \* \*

Percy Newton Corry in his **'The Quire and Misericords of St Mary's Parish Church, Nantwich, Cheshire, 1974'**, tells us whilst discussing the misericord which he, and later Francis Blackley in 1998, believed to be Richard II; and which evidence above certainly suggests this to be the case: that *"Richard II himself was in Nantwich in August, 1398, because on the 31st of that month, John Cranmere, yeoman of the King's wardrobe, (Chester Recognisance Rolls) obtained a receipt for "two carpets of red tapestry and a green mattress, being part of the Royal furniture which had been left behind at Nantwich."* And also that *"on the 21st of August, 1399 Richard stayed yet again in Nantwich on his last journey to London where before his disposition on September 23rd, he issued his commission constituting "Richard de Vernon, of Shipbroke; Thomas de Fouleshurst of Edlaston; Richard de Roop; Tho de Maisterson; Richard Massey and William Crew, Keepers of the Peace for the Hundred of Wich Malbank". It is interesting to see that all these names belonged to gentlemen of this town and its immediate neighbourhood. This* *was probably the last warrant issued by Richard's authority and in his name."*

\* \* \* \* \* \* \*

The reason we have little historic documentary evidence of the building of St Mary's, and who its main benefactors and patrons were, may be due to Cheshire nobles being enemies of Henry IV, who deposed their King, Richard II. Henry fought many rebellions in Cheshire, whose nobles supported the opposing heirs to the throne, and these rebellions were suppressed with difficulty. It probably served the longevity of the monuments of St Mary's, and its fabric, to possibly later destroy the records that it was most likely finished by Richard II, Henry's enemy, on behalf of his father the Black Prince, and his grandfather, Edward III, and the local nobility opposed to King Henry IV.

In 1399 Henry Bollingbroke, the later Henry IV, takes Chester when it surrendered without a fight, and later captures Richard II at Flint two weeks later, who he imprisons for a few days in Chester Castle.

In 1400 Richard's supporters in Cheshire, revolted against the usurper Henry, and besieged Chester Castle, but were unsuccessful.[70]

King Richard, albeit deposed, died in mysterious circumstances in prison at Pontefract Castle, West Yorkshire. He is thought to have been starved to death, on or around 14 February 1400.

However, the deposing of Richard II caused the ensuing Wars of the Roses, with Cheshire men fighting for their believed true heirs to the throne of England. The nobility of Cheshire and their men at arms, including their famous archers, took part in the Battle of Shrewsbury in 1403, and then later the Battle of Blore Heath in 1459.

The quick end to Richard II's reign may have been the reason why some parts of St Mary's were left unfinished, especially if the Lady Chapel and Crossing stone vaults were never in fact completed.

\* \* \* \* \* \* \*

The destruction of the records of St Mary's and Combermere may have proved necessary, because much of Cheshire was destroyed by Henry IV's soldiers, and he confiscated much of the lords of Cheshire's lands.

Unless of course, we owe the lack of documentation to the time of the mid 17$^{th}$ century English Civil War, when St Mary's was used as stables, and later as a prison to house Royalist soldiers, after Parliament's victory to lift the siege of the town, at the Battle of Nantwich, on 25 January 1644. It is believed that some of the damage to the alabaster effigy of Sir David Cradock, Knight (see later), occurred at this time.

Or maybe the best reason we only have documentation surviving from 1538, when the Abbey of Combermere was taken by Henry VIII in the Dissolution of the Monasteries, is because the records disappeared or were destroyed in the fateful process.

This is reinforced in the **'Introduction, The Book of the Abbot of Combermere: 1289 to 1529, Edited by James Hall, The Record Society of Lancashire and Cheshire, Volume 31, 1896, Page 1'**, where we are told: *"that the [majority of] Combermere [Abbey's historic] records disappeared or perished before the 17$^{th}$ century"*.

\* \* \* \* \* \* \*

It is interesting to note, that Eric Garton in his **'Nantwich: Saxon to Puritan, 1972, Pages 23 & 24'**, tells us that:-

> "On the 24 January 1397/8 King Richard II, personally, at his court at Westminster [Public Record Office, C86/345/m 29.] appointed John Inglewode to the "deanery church of Nantwich" on the false suggestion by Inglewode that the place was vacant and that the king had the right to appoint. The Abbot of Combermere, Thomas Bernewell, objected and on the 15 May 1398 the court of Chancery cancelled the appointment, agreeing with the abbot's assertion the church at Nantwich had been held by him and his predecessors from time immemorial as a chapel annexed to the church of Acton. The sheriff of London issued a warrant for the arrest of John Inglewode, but he was never found."

Surely if the King felt he had the power to appoint a Dean of St Mary's, then Richard II must have been so inextricably linked with the Church; and near its completion year, and the appointment of its Dean, over that of the control of Combermere Abbey, which was then overturned, and that it was also rather fortuitous that the man he wanted to preside over the church, and had given him evidence of his right to appoint him; went missing?

We know from **'Royal Administration of Cheshire Abbeys in the Late Middle Ages, Ann J Kettle, Cheshire History, Volume 4, 1979 Autumn, Pages 43 – 54'**, that Combermere Abbey had often been in royal custody, especially during the $13^{th}$ century, and a few times during the $14^{th}$ century. This was due to financial difficulties, mismanagement, or sometimes the cost of unwelcome hospitality. The Abbot and Abbey were afforded royal protection for two years in 1383. This may be why Nantwich Church, which was part of the Abbey's holdings, had royal patronage, and why Richard II felt able to overrule the Abbey with the appointing of a Dean, due to the royal expenditure on the church.

Nantwich's octagonal tower may also be indicative of the link with Richard II, who was born and known as 'of Bordeaux', with the Abbey at Grand-Sauve near the French city, also having an octagonal tower. Sir David Cradock, his friend, was also the Mayor of Bordeaux. So the link between Bordeaux and Nantwich is a strong one (see earlier details).

# Sir David Cradock, Knight
# Friend of King Richard II
# Founder of Nantwich (St Mary's) Church?

Sir David Cradock, was a Knight: whose medieval alabaster effigy still exists in the South Transept, of the Chapel of St Nicholas (before known as the 'Kingsley Chapel'), in Nantwich St Mary's, albeit damaged and graffitied in antiquity, atop a replica of his original chest tomb: who came from the town; was Justice of North Wales in 1373, and between July 1376 and June 1377; and was the Mayor of Bordeaux; as well as a money-lender to King Richard II; and who died around the 1380s, at the same time St Mary's was being rebuilt, is thought to be the founder of this 14$^{th}$ century church.[71]

His coat of arms consisted of a silver shield with a blue chevron, upon which were three golden wheat sheaves. His crest was a black bear's head with a red muzzle.

Sir David Cradock was very likely a friend of King Richard II, as well as being his money-lender. For David to be made Mayor of Bordeaux suggests this, as King Richard was born there, and was often known as 'Richard of Bordeaux'. We also know that he served and was a friend of Edward the Black Prince, King Richard's father (see above and below).

A fellow man from Nantwich, Sir Nicholas Colfox, Knight (see above), was also the friend of the King and was thought to have taken part in the murder of Thomas of Woodstock, the hated uncle of the King, and it is thought he acted on behalf of the throne, and evaded justice, most likely due to his kingly friendship.

David is believed to have been the son of Nicholas Cradock and Alice, who are believed to have married c1341, and to have lived at some point at Weston, to the east of Nantwich.[72]

Eric Garton tells us in his **'Nantwich: Saxon to Puritan, 1972, Page 13'**, that:-

> *"Where young David Cradock received his education cannot be said, or when he went to London, presumably to study laws, perhaps at Chesters Inn, otherwise called Strand Inn, outside the city of London. This Inn existed until 1411.*
>
> *David evidently acquired knowledge of the workings of the Law as J[u]n[e]. 1356 he was one of four men appointed by Roger Cradock, Bishop of Water-ford, to act as his attorney(1). Another of the four men was Roger de Wyche, who may, also, have been from Nantwich.*
>
> *Although David witnessed a lease of land and buildings in Nantwich which had belonged to Margery de Sonde, on the 1st November 1360, he evidently lived in London at the time, as before 13th November he had surrendered himself to the Keeper of the Fleet Prison, having heard that, in his absence, he had been outlawed for not attending before the justices of the bench to answer a plea of debt of 20 marks, made by Henry Comyn(2). A certificate having been given to the Chief Justice by the Keeper of the Fleet Prison that David Cradock had surrendered himself, he was pardoned at the Husting held at the Guildhall of London on the 13th November 1360."*

David is believed to have married a lady named Ireland in about 1362.[73] He had three children, Pelerine, Richard, and Roger.

Eric Garton also stated that David Cradock would have spent most of his working life outside of Nantwich, and likewise did his son, Richard.[74] This is certainly apparent when we remember he served in Wales and was later Justice of Wales, although he may have spent some time whilst officiating in that office in Nantwich and Chester.

We also know that David Cradock bought land in Nantwich, which was situated between Nantwich Castle's remaining motte, and the High Street, and above Waterlode leading to the river, on 29 May 1362.[75] He also held some land in Hospital Street, which he sold to Richard de Godwynslegh.[76]

Eric Garton also tells us that the Black Prince granted an income of £40 a year for life to be paid to David Cradock for his services in Wales on 30 May 1374. This was confirmed again by Richard of Bordeaux, the future King Richard II, Edward the Black Prince's son, when he became Prince of Wales and held the Earldom of Chester.[77]

David would also have been in residence at the castles of North Wales, such as Conway, Caernarvon, and Harlech.

As Justice of Wales, he would have had a large retinue of men at arms as well as archers, to protect the claim to Wales by the Kings of England. Based at the castles of North Wales, both major and minor, he would have led or sent out, parties of men to subdue any violent skirmishes or attacks led by the Welsh. This would have honed the skills of the men at arms, and the Cheshire Archers, who would most likely see at some point battle in France, in the Hundred Years' War.

After trouble in Wales, in 1379 he was made the Mayor of Bordeaux. He held this office until 1384 or 1389.[78]

His tomb was referred to in February 1711, as a monument, which may have been much larger and prominent before the 19th and 20th century renovations of St Mary's. A description of the tomb tells us that it *"was an altar-tomb of red stone, the sides being ornamented with shields included in quatre-foils. On the top was the recumbent figure of the Knight in alabaster, habited in plate armour, with conical helmet and gorget of mail; his hands clasped on his breast and a sword by his side. The legs were not crossed; the feet rested on a lion, and the head reposed on the crest, which was the head of a lamb. We are also told that he was 'the Founder [of the Church]'"*.[79]

It is also interesting that according to the above '**Rental of lands belonging to the Knights and Hospitallers of St. John of Jerusalem and of the lands of Robert Salamon, Nantwich area, c.1380-1390 (CALS Ref: DDX350)'**, Lord Richard Crado[c]k, Knight, held land in Nantwich, which was in the tenure of Richard Girdy, from the Knights Hospitaller.

Sir David is also recorded as gifting all his lands, tenements, and rents in Nantwich, on 8 July 1366, to Sir Nicholas de Haselynton [Haslington], Chaplain.[80] Whether this was a gift of some of his property to the Church early in his career, we may never know, but he certainly held property in Nantwich, and elsewhere after this date. Whether Sir Nicholas de Haslington, Chaplain, was a knight and chaplain of the Order of the Knights Hospitaller we cannot be sure, but it may also be possible.

Sir Richard Cradock, Knight, was the heir of Sir David Cradock, Knight. Richard also had a brother called Roger.[81] They also inherited all his lands and tenements in Nantwich and other areas of Cheshire and England, which due to them not producing male heirs, were ultimately inherited by Pelerine, their older sister.[82]

Richard had been taken prisoner after fighting the French at Ypres in 1383, during a Crusade against them. Sir Hugh Calveley accompanied Richard, whose tomb and effigy sits in St Bonifice's Church at Bunbury. He had also taken part in the battles but had not been captured. David had to raise money to pay the ransom for his son to be released, 300 gold francs of which was received from the Abbot of the Abbey of Sainte Croix de Bordeaux, with the assistance of Raymond de Roqueys, Archbishop of the French city.[83] Richard went on to have an illustrious career and was knighted, like his father.

David also took as a ward, whilst Justice of Wales, John de Olton, the 5-year-old son of Randulph de Olton, deceased. John had been born at the manor house of Erdeswick and baptised at Church Minshull in 1371. John had been married to David's eldest child, Pelerine. They had three daughters, named Elenor, Jane, and Margarett. John died aged 25, on 9 October 1396. Pelerine remarried to Robert Massy of Aldford (and later of Hale), and had a son Thomas.[84]

**The Tomb and Effigy of Sir David Cradock, Knight, in the South Transept of St Mary's Church, Nantwich**

\* \* \* \* \* \* \*

Sir David Cradock who is believed to be the reputed founder of Nantwich's 14th century St Mary's, and his links with Edward III, Edward the Black Prince, and Richard II, must certainly be such, and must have had grants of money from them as well as Royal Patronage, to construct such a magnificent edifice, and to record such personal Royal links in stone and wood.

His grandfather is said to have provided stone for the building of Vale Royal Abbey in 1288,[85] another building with links to Edward III, the Black Prince, and Richard II.

Mark Downing, a leading authority on all military church monuments between 1200 and 1500, in England and Wales, in his talk **'Military Effigies of the Yorkist Age, The Churches Conservation Trust, YouTube, 24 August 2021'**, tells us that:-

> "People ask the question: "Do effigies bear a likeness of the deceased?" and the answer is no. Only a very small proportion of what survives, do we think [that] there is any [actual] portrayal."

Mark Downing believes that alabaster effigies were mass produced by dedicated workshops, and that is why the great majority are stereotypical. These workshops had to be kept busy and could not wait for individual contracts, as well as the fact that a large number of knights were dying suddenly in the wars of the 14$^{th}$ and 15$^{th}$ century period. Sculptors at these workshops would have just rolled out as many as they could, to meet the demand. All but the most extravagant of nobles, or royals, ever really had the money and time to commission funerary effigies which actually bore a resemblance to their likenesses.

The alabaster effigy of Sir David Cradock sadly is rather damaged (left), but it doesn't really match any of St Mary's Tower sculptured stone royal patrons. It doesn't really have any remains of flowing hair or beard, even if it wasn't a stereotypical likeness. Neither did his two sons die before him to face an owl in stone, showing that they had been taken far too soon.

This then suggests if Sir David Cradock had spent a fortune of his own money building and founding the ornate and lavishly exquisitely detailed 14$^{th}$ century church of Nantwich, and the royals were not involved, or others, then why did he not have a massively lavish memorial, like that for Sir William Mainwaring of Baddiley and Peover, at nearby St Mary's Church at Acton, who died at a similar time, in 1399, than this rather simple alabaster effigy on a stone chest tomb? It may possibly have had a canopy originally, and may have originally stood in the Chancel, or possibly in the 'Old Treasury / Sacristy' once nicknamed the 'Old Crypt', as a personal Chantry Chapel.

However, he likely wasn't the greatest purse to the building of St Mary's, but was likely the main benefactor of the church, and wherever his body laid, it is more than likely he was watched over by his fellow patrons, his Royal friends and rulers, who also looked over the townsfolk worshipping within its sacred walls, for time immemorial, "Hidden in Plain Sight", until that which was lost was found again!

# The Priory
# &
# The Hospital and Chapel of St Lawrence
# (Welsh Row, Nantwich)

There was also another medieval hospital which was thought to be situated at the head of Welsh Row, supposedly near to the Almshouses, to the immediate south-east of Malbank School, which was known as the Hospital of St Lawrence, and had a Chapel associated with it. It lay in or next to Acton St Mary's Parish.

According to previous research and historic documents, of which few records survive, this hospital was a house for sufferers of leprosy, who were not entitled to enter the town, to its east, and therefore it existed to Nantwich's western boundary.

Leprosy and the fear of catching it, made folk live in terror of the disease, and therefore the hospital would have had a distinct precinct, to keep the sufferers away from anyone travelling through Nantwich and via the main road past the hospital.

The hospital had a well associated with it, dedicated to St Lawrence. Water was associated with the healing of the disease, and sufferers would wash by the well, or use the water taken from it. Leper hospitals also often had their own water source, due to the fear of spreading the disease and contaminating water sources used by others.

The leper hospital later became a hospital for the housing of those of ill health and the poor.

We also know that the records tell us that it had a Chapel, whose first recorded chaplain was John Fowler, appointed in 1499. The hospital chaplain would have officiated in divine service for the people it housed.

St Lawrence's wasn't controlled by a religious house, and its associated chapel was often referred to as a 'Free Chapel'. This means that it was either separately controlled, or that it was part of a secular order which was separate from Church or Monastic control. This meant that it was in the care of a secular clerk, i.e. a chaplain. The chaplain might also be the Prior, Master, or Warden of the hospital, charged with the duties of running the institution, officiating over the ill people housed within, both in a spiritual and caring manner, along with a number of laymen he would have presided over. Often the chaplains or masters would have held other offices in the locality or elsewhere, but whilst not present at the hospital, they would have left it in the charge of brethren, sisters, novices, and lay folk.

* * * * * * *

The first historical source which relates to lepers in Nantwich, appears in the Wilbraham Manuscripts at Cheshire Archives & Local Studies (CALS Ref: DWN/1/1), where we find in a Lease for 22 years, by Hugh son of Geoffrey cum Naso [with the Nose] to Laurence Cok' de Chester, clerk [of holy orders], of the messuage with land, held from William son of Matthew, in the vill of Wych Mauban [Wych Malbank, i.e. Nantwich], at a yearly rent of 6d, and a sester [approx 1.25 to 1.67 pints] from each brewing brewed on the said land, is to go to the **'lepers of Wych Mauban'**, for 1d, taken from the said lepers. Also, that the said Laurence, his heirs, and assigns, are allowed within the said term, to sell or remove the building which Hugh had built there. The consideration (lease fee) was 6 marks of silver.

This lease dates to 25 April 1260 and may be the first reference to a possible leper house in Nantwich. It seems likely the reason why the messuage and land (the property) being leased; and the building Hugh cum Naso had built there (which the deed includes may be sold or removed), had a clause to provide beer at the price of 1d (beer was the usual drink for the lower classes in the medieval period rather than water), for the lepers of Nantwich; was because a leper colony was associated with the property.

This historic deed also includes the brewing of beer, which needs a good supply of water. St Lawrence's Well was part of the hospital complex, whose water was used for the lepers to wash with.

Could Geoffrey cum Naso [with the Nose] have been a sufferer of leprosy, his name certainly suggests this?

Also interesting is the leaser's name, 'Laurence' Cok' of Chester, who was a clerk, meaning a religious cleric or clergyman, who may have possibly founded or first named St Laurence's / Lawrence's [Leper] Hospital and Chapel, after himself and the patron saint of his name. This may indicate that he was linked with its early beginnings, being part of the religious establishment of Cheshire, nearly a century before the Hospital is mentioned by name in historical documents.

Interestingly, in **'A History of the Church of Saint Mary, Nantwich: to the Dissolution of The Monasteries, 1536, Francis Blacklay, 1998'**, we are told that Laurence Cok de Chester, was believed to be the clerk of Nantwich St Mary's in c1275 to c1285.

According to **'Nantwich: Saxon to Puritan, A History of the Hundred of Nantwich, 1050 to 1642, Eric Garton, 1972, Page 9'**, we are told that an Inquisition dating to 1354-5 says that:-

> *"The jurors say that Acton by Nantwich and the hospital of St. Lawrence were bound to provide a chaplain or priest to sing divine service each day, and to provide three hospital beds to receive the infirm poor until they recover their health; which service is withdrawn, four years having elapsed and the value now is 20 shillings per annum; in testimony of which, etc.,"(which is taken and translated from the Latin text of the Inquisition contained within the footnotes of* **'Ormerod's History of Cheshire: Volume 3, Page 450')***"*

This tells us that by the mid 14th century St Lawrence's was no longer operating as a leper hospital, but instead housed those of ill health, and of poor means.

Eric Garton goes on to say:-

> *"This shows the hospital to have been in the parish of Acton and to have been supported by that parish and its own tithes. Neither the name of the founder nor the name of the holder of the advowson is known, except that one third of*

*the advowson was held by Lord Lovell. The absence of an incumbent and his services in 1350 suggests the Black Death took its toll.*

*Towards the end of the fifteenth century the property belonged to the Audley fee and a chaplain or master was provided. It passed to the Crown after the Perkin Warbeck rebellion."*

According to **'Notitia Cestriensis or Historical Notices of the Diocese of Chester, Rev. Francis Gastrell, Bishop of Chester (c1720), with notes by Rev. F. R. Raines, Volume I: Cheshire, The Chetham Society, First Series, Volume 8, 1845, Page 224'**, the Chapel [and Hospital] of St Lawrence in 1488/89, during the reign of Henry VII, along with an appurtenant (hereditary part) of the Barony, was forfeited from Francis Lord Lovell after the battle of Stoke, and granted, inter alia (among other things), to Sir William Stanley (chamberlain of Chester), the sixth part of the Barony of Wich-Malbank, (and the advowson of the Chapel of St Nicholas), and also the third part of the Chapel of St Lawrence.[86]

\* \* \* \* \* \* \*

We know from **'A History of the County of Chester: Volume 3, Victoria County History, 1980, Page 186'**, that the Masters or Chaplains of St Lawrence's Chapel and Hospital, from 1499 to 1545 were:-

| Hospital Master | Years | Source |
| --- | --- | --- |
| John Fowler | appointed 1499 | *Cal. Pat.* 14941509, 164. He was a clerk of the royal chapel and was appointed by the king who held the advowson after the attainder of James, Lord Audley in 1497. |
| John Incent, B.C.L. [Bachelor in Canon Law] | occurs 1535 | *Valor Eccl.* (Rec. Com.), v. 218. For his career and benefices see Emden, *Biog. Reg. Oxford*, ii. 999. |
| Richard Wright | occurs 1545 | *Lancs. & Ches. Rec.* ii (R.S.L.C. viii), 395 |
| **DISSOLVED: 1548** | | |

In an Inquisition dating to 1529/30, in the reign of Henry VIII, on the forfeiture of Sir William Stanley, Knight, finds *"that he held the manor and vill of Wich Malbank in fee, with its appurtenances [hereditary lands] in Cow-lane, Newhall, Copenhale, Wolstanwood, and Acton, with the Chapel of St. Nicholas, and the third part of the Chapel of St. Lawrence"*.[87]

The other two-thirds of the advowson of the Chapel and Hospital of St Lawrence belonged in the 15th century, to the Audley family.

According to **'The History of Cheshire, Volume 3, George Ormerod, 1882, Page 450'**, in the Ecclesiastical Survey of 1534-35, the Chapel of St Laurence's Master was Doctor [John] Incent. It also tells us that Richard Wrighte, in 1556, is recorded in the pension roll as the incumbent of the Chapel of St James (which existed at the old Castle of Newhall, near to Combermere Abbey) annexed with the Chapel of St Lawrence, and receiving an income of 68 shillings and 4 pence a year.

St Lawrence's Chapel and Hospital was dissolved at the time of the Dissolution of the Monasteries, in 1548. At this time it was valued at 76 shillings a year, and had bells valued at 2 shillings, but no silver plate, jewels, goods, ornaments, or lead.

Due to the Hospital being referred to as a Chapel or Chantry in its later history (i.e. in the 16th century), it most likely ended its life just as a free chapel, rather than a place to house the ill and poor, as a hospital.

According to **'Nantwich: Saxon to Puritan, Eric Garton, Pages 66-67'**, and the **'Calendar of Patent Rolls, 7 September 1548, m 57 & 59'**: *"on the 7th September 1548 to William Warde, gentleman of London and Richard Venables Esquire, sergeant at arms"*, was granted *"three cottages, 2 gardens, 2 salt houses of 6 lead[pan]s each, and nine pieces of land called "le nine Buttes" in the hospytall croft". This grant also gave William Warde and Richard Venables the sites of the late free Chapel of St. Lawrence and the late Chapel of St. James in Newall, both in the parish of Acton; the two crofts of land called St. Lawrence croft and "le chapel croft", half another little croft, two salthouses belonging to the free chapels and all possessions of the chapels Richard Wright being the tenant."*

This, therefore, tells us the owners of these properties after they were dissolved, including St Lawrence's Chapel, as well as its two namesake fields, and that Richard Wright was the tenant.

Detailed during the reign of Edward VI (1547-1553) the *"Frechappell of Sent Laurens and Sent James [A lazar hospital in Welsh Row.] in the toune"*, was appraised at a yearly value of 76 shillings.[88]

St Lawrence's Chapel was also some time before the Dissolution annexed with the Chapel of St James in Newhall (near Aston), located where the Audley family's Castle or Peel/Pele Tower and Hall was located, which controlled the Nantwich to Whitchurch / Shrewsbury road, and the crossing of the nearby watercourse. This defensive site along with its associated chapel was located to the immediate north-west of the industrial bakery.

We are told in a 1588 Grant, that the *"lands late of the chantry within the chapel of Namptwicham [Nantwich]"* and the *"chapel of St Lawrence, Nantwich"* were transferred from: William and Thomas Kirkham, of Gray's Inn, Middlesex, Gentlemen; to Thomas Tettnall of Tattenhall, Gentleman.[89] This, therefore implies that St Lawrence's Chapel was still standing, or at least the land associated with it remained, in 1588.

Again in an Indenture of Sale, dated 1590, we are told William and Thomas Kirkham, of Gray's Inn, etc, sells to John Mere, of Mere, Cheshire, Esq., and Henry More, of Weley, Cheshire, servant to John Mere, the *"land sometime belonging to the late chantry in the chapel of Namptwicham, Cheshire" "and the chapel in Nantwiche called St. Laurence Chappell, Cheshire"*,[90] which again suggests that St Lawrence's Chapel and its associated land was still extant in 1590.

We are told in **'An Historical Account of the Town and Parish of Nantwich, Joseph Partridge, 1774, Pages 8-9'**, that "*At the end of this street [Welsh Row] leading to Chester, the Abbot and Monks of the Abb[e]y of Combermere, who were the order of St. Benedict [actually Cistercian, but living under the rule of St Benedict] erected a Priory, but no marks or footsteps thereof have remained for perhaps some centuries past, but the arms said to belong thereto, are noticed by King in his Vale Royal, which are*

*Party per Pale, Azure and Gules, two crutches in Saltier Or. There was likewise an Hospital or Lazar House, called St. Laurences's Hospital termed in several deeds, Domus Leprosorum, near the Priory, (if it was distinct from it, for some suppose them both the same) and the arms seem to countenance [support] that opinion, nevertheless, I apprehend they are mistaken, for to me the existence of both erections seem indisputable. A Priory or Lazar House are different things; the existence of the latter is fully proved by several deeds yet extant, and what is called the Prior's Obitt [actually the Praer's family Obitt, and not related], is collected by the Parish Officers to this day, it is generally agreed that they (if distinct edifices) were situated over against the Alms Houses, founded and endowed by the very worthy and ancient family of Wilbraham. There is an ancient tradition which holds that the priory was built upon the site, upon a part of which, now stands the Malt House occupied by Mr. Bayley, very near the said Alms Houses, now this is almost opposite the other situation, and if tradition could be depended upon would be a further proof that the Priory and Lazar House could not be one, but distinct edifices; in all probability the Hospital or Lazar House, might be under the inspection of the Prior and his Monks."*

And according to **'The History and Antiquities of Nantwich, in the County Palatine of Chester, J.W. Platt, 1818, Pages 22-25':-**

> *"The Priory.*
> *The Abbot and Monks, of the Abbey of Combermere, belonging to the order of Cistertians, erected, at the end of the Welsh Row, leading to Chester, a priory; but no traces thereof have been discovered for many centuries back. The celebrated Mr. King, in his Vale Royal, notices the arms which are said to have belonged to it, as being "per pale, azure, and gules, two crutches in saltier or.*
>
> *Lazar - House.*
> *Opposite to the priory was situated the lazar house, called St. Laurence's Hospital; though, in several deeds, it is stiled Domus Leprosorum. The site of these buildings is a disputed point; many gentlemen have entered the lists, and displayed considerable acuteness in the logical disposition of their arguments. As far as I have been enabled to investigate the*

*disputed point, they have darkened, rather than elucidated the subject. It has been generally supposed, but upon what authority, I know not, that the priory and lazar-house were one. In my opinion, they are two very different places. The one is a house for the reception of the diseased;*

*If I mistake not, but I speak from memory, what is called the Prior's obiit, is collected in the parish to the present time. There is a tradition, which places the site of the priory, where the present alms-houses are erected. Upon the same evidence, the lazar house was exactly opposite the priory. Were it possible to produce any well-attested document, sanctioning in the least, this tradition, it would be a further proof that the priory and lazar-house could not possibly be one, but distinct edifices. When I consider the nature of a priory and lazar house, I am more willing to pronounce them two distinct edifices, than to fall into the common error of classing them under one head. It is possible, that both the priory and lazar-house were under the governance of the Prior; which circumstance may, in conjunction with the supposed arms, have produced the erroneous conclusion."*

These details, therefore tell us that it was believed in the late 18th and early 19th centuries, by the first two Nantwich historians, that at the head of Welsh Row, St Lawrence's Hospital existed next to a Priory, or on the opposite side of the road to a Priory, of which nothing, even back then was really known. Partridge tells us that the Priory was most likely in the vicinity of the later almshouses, and likely once existed on the site of the later Malthouse, with the Lazar House (St Lawrence's Hospital) either next door or on the opposite side of the road.

Over time these two separate entities have been mixed together somewhat, to confuse the situation further, even by modern writers.

We do know though from historic conjecture over the centuries, that a priory had existed somewhere on Welsh Row, and also that Combermere Abbey was thought to have had a monastic cell in Nantwich, so could these be the same as the Priory Partridge and Platt elude to?

\* \* \* \* \* \* \*

According to **'Notitia Cestriensis or Historical Notices of the Diocese of Chester, Rev. Francis Gastrell, Bishop of Chester (c1720), with notes by Rev. F. R. Raines, Volume I: Cheshire, The Chetham Society, First Series, Volume 8, 1845, Page 86'**, we are told that there was a "**Namptwych Priory[1]: Prior** of Namptwich one of ye Spirituall Barons to H.[ugh] Lupus E.[arl] of Chester. M[anu]S[cript]. Crew[e Family]. [Footnote 1 by Rev. F. R. Raines: This was probably a Cell to Combermere, and not a distinct religious foundation. Nothing is known of any Priory here.]"

Cheshire Archives & Local Studies description of Bishop Gastrell's **'Notitia Cestriensis'**, tells us that "*The Notitia result from an extensive survey undertaken by Francis Gastrell (bishop 1714-25) to establish the rights and responsibilities of the diocese and comprise, for each parish or chapelry, notes on value of the living, patronage, sources of revenue, population, recusancy, schools and charities etc. These are arranged by archdeaconry, deanery and parish.*"

This, therefore adds another earlier historic reference in around 1720 which includes that the details came from a once-existing manuscript of the Crewe Family, to a priory at Nantwich, or at least some sort of monastic establishment most likely linked to Combermere Abbey. This is about half a century before Partridge mentions anything about a priory existing at Nantwich.

Also according to the Armorial Bearings featured in **'The Vale Royal of England, Daniel King, 1656'**, 'Namptwich Priory' had a coat of arms "*Per pale Azure [Blue] and Gules [Red] [two colours eitherside of a central line running vertically through the shield] two palmers' staves (croziers) [pilgrim's staffs] in saltire [in an 'X' shape] [in] Or [Gold]*".

We are also told by the **'Nantwich Chronicle, Saturday 17th September 1955, Page 12'**, under the article '*Forerunner of the Modern "Barony" – First Nantwich hospital dates from William the Conqueror*', that an interesting shield (coat of arms) is depicted by the Elizabethan antiquary [William] Smith in his "Alphabet of Armoury." This book is said to depict this "*coat of arms emblazons two crutches crossed in saltire (or) on a parti-coloured background* *(per pale gules and azure). This purported to belong to a cell of Combermere Abbey at Nantwich."* Although the article suggests that this shield refers to St Nicholas' Hospital, is unlikely, because this was not in fact controlled by the Abbot of Combermere or any monastic or ecclesiastical order, because it is often recorded as a Free Chapel with its own chaplain, as likewise, St Lawrence's Chapel was, and the former was most likely owned ultimately, by the Knights Hospitaller. If St Nicholas' had a coat of arms, it would surely be similar to the Maltese Cross of the Hospitallers, and not have contained crutches.

This original book is held by the College of Arms, and is titled **'Alphabet or Blazon of Arms, by William Smith, 1597'**. This record dates to 59 years before **'The Vale Royal of England, 1656'**, see above.

***The Coat of Arms of Namptwich Priory (left)
and of Combermere Abbey (right)***
***Attribution:*** *Rcsprinter123, CC BY 3.0
<https://creativecommons.org/licenses/by/3.0>, via Wikimedia Commons
(**Source:** https://commons.wikimedia.org/wiki/File:Map_of_Cheshire_1923.jpg)*

Taken from a 1923 Map of Cheshire, albeit with the Combermere Abbey coat of arms shown with an upright incorrect bishop's staff, or crozier, rather than the correct depiction of a gold crozier sitting diagonally across the shield, from bottom left to top right, are the two shields of both religious establishments.

The coat of arms of this priory are similar to those of Combermere Abbey, which according to the *'Monasticon Anglicanum, William Dugdale, 1825, Page 322'*, *"were those of the founder, Hugh de Malbanc, (quarterly, Or [Gold] and Gules [Red], a bendlet [a bend or band or strap half as wide as just a bend or band, running from the upper corner on the left, of the shield to the lower curved right side] Sa[ble]. [Black]) debruised [cut diagonally] by a crozier [Bishops Staff] in pale Or [Gold], the head turned sinister-ways [to the left hand side]".*

However, they are not that similar and this may mean the Priory wasn't actually linked with the Abbot and monks of the Cistercian Abbey of Combermere, and may actually relate to another monastic foundation.

It may be that the coat of arms of the Priory, with its crossed pilgrim's staffs, may in fact relate to the Crossed / Crutched / or Crozier Friars, which may be linked with the Guild of the Holy Cross, which we know are linked with St Mary's Church of Nantwich, and its once standing Guildhall in the Churchyard, and the medieval hospital at Wybunbury, which was known as the Hospital of the Holy Cross and St George.

The Crossed / Crutched / or Crozier Friars were a religious order in England and Ireland. Their symbol was a staff surmounted by a cross, which is certainly similar to the Priory's coat of arms. They were known to hold medieval hospitals, and look after the poor, ill of health, and the elderly.

Please see the final chapter for further discussion of this religious order(s).

\* \* \* \* \* \* \*

The detail in *'The Vale Royal of England, Daniel King, 1656'*, dates to some 64 years before Bishop Gastrell's account in c1720, and the *'Alphabet or Blazon of Arms, William Smith, 1597'*, dates to some 123 years before Gastrell's account, and reveals to us that Nantwich Priory was connected with a place for pilgrims, i.e. it presumably gave pilgrims hospitality, i.e. food, drink and shelter, whilst travelling, as well as presumably being a house for the poor, ill of health, and destitute. Much the same as abbeys, priories, and hospitals, did across the country, and where the original form of the word 'hotel' derives from, a hostel, or hospice, i.e. a hospital, and hospitality.

This is in the same guise as Combermere Abbey, St Nicholas's Hospital in Nantwich, as well as St Lawrence's Hospital (which later in its life was no longer used for the treatment of lepers, but for the infirm and poor), operated, as recorded in historic records, when the gentry/knights and their entourage, took advantage of this hospitality when essentially it was meant for the poor, pilgrims, and those of lesser means travelling the country, and those requiring care, to be housed.

The supposed site of Nantwich Priory at the head of Welsh Row, and St Nicholas' Hospital at the other end of the town, at the eastern end of the street which acquired its name from the Hospital, i.e. Hospital Street, are on the same main road through the town of Nantwich, and situated on opposite sides of the River Weaver. They are also on a major routeway between London and the City of Chester, and situated on an important pilgrimage route to St Werburgh's Shrine and Abbey, in Chester, which is now known as Chester Cathedral. Thus both religious establishments were perfect for the travelling pilgrims, when both existed (although the Priory may have been short-lived, due to the lack of historic evidence available, or the records like those for the building of St Mary's Church were likely destroyed at the Dissolution), and would have been perfectly situated at the east and west entrances to the town.

The crossed palmer's staves or pilgrim's staffs are certainly linked with the act of pilgrimage, and many hospitals up and down the country gave pilgrims hospitality during their journeys.

As well as the important shrine in Chester of St Werburgh; St John's Church by the Amphitheatre, also in Chester, St Mary's at Acton, as well as Vale Royal Abbey, had pieces of the True Cross housed in their sanctuaries. A Priory or Hospital for the use of pilgrims would have been perfect for those travelling to these shrines, on this main route through Nantwich, to and from Chester and London.

Religious relics, especially those linked with the life and time of Christ, certainly benefitted the Mother Church massively, and the holy orders that held these relics in their respective houses of God raised much-needed revenue for their orders.

The Priory would, like many monastic houses, possibly in this case, Combermere, prove a worthy investment, originally (and before this hospitality was abused, see below), to establish these religious houses or hospitals for pilgrims, and in the latter case, also for the poor and infirm, or their rich benefactors, would raise money for their ruling religious houses, and their day-to-day running, by way of care and more lucratively, providing food, drink and shelter. Likewise, those paying or being charitable for their received hospitality; would also be raising money for the care of those also housed in the hospital, due to ill health, age, or because of their poor circumstances.

As we saw above, the abuse of the Abbey's hospitality is revealed in **'Cheshire Under the Three Edwards. A History of Cheshire, Volume 5, H. J. Hewitt, 1967, Page 92'**, where we are told that the abbey was one of four monastic houses to complain to Edward, the Black Prince in 1351, about the costs it was accruing due to providing hospitality to guests and their servants, horses and hunting hounds.

And in **'Wrenbury and Marbury, Local History Group, F. A. Latham (editor), 1999, Page 24'**, it is speculated that because of the abbey's proximity to the road from Chester to Shrewsbury, meant that the cost of its hospitality to travellers was a drain on its resources.

* * * * * * *

It is quite possible that the establishment referred to as 'Namptwich Priory' in the historic records, and as the crossed crutches or pilgrim's staffs on its coat of arms allude to, was actually in the business of looking after the ill of health and the poor, as well as those on pilgrimage, much the same as St Nicholas', and St Lawrence's in its later history, which would mean it was more of a hospital than a priory.

If so this makes the picture even more difficult of separating both establishments located at the Head of Welsh Row.

It may be possible that after St Lawrence's Hospital no longer served sufferers of leprosy, its 'hospital hall or infirmary' was rebuilt on the other side of the road, to that of the Chapel, of which we have evidence, stood on the south side of Welsh Row, see later. When a leprosy hospital, it would have had a distinct boundary to separate the sufferers, in isolation from travellers on the adjacent roadway, so would certainly have not been established on both sides of the road, originally.

The term Priory may relate to a religious order, like the 'Priory of St John' or the Hospitallers (see above chapters), like St Nicholas' on the other side of the town. Both may have been established for pilgrims travelling through Nantwich, unlike the original leper hospital but the later medieval hospital opposite. However, the coat of arms of the Priory certainly doesn't reflect any link to the Hospitallers.

\* \* \* \* \* \* \*

If not for pilgrims, was it for the conducting of estate business by Combermere Abbey, as **'Monastic and Collegiate Cheshire, Roland W. Morant, 1996, Page 80'** suggests, where we are told that *"Ormerod [1872, Vol. III, P. 450] recalls a local tradition that a distinct religious foundation which apparently was a cell of Combermere abbey, existed at the end of Welsh Row in that town [Nantwich] to which the name, 'The Priory', was given in old records and which was erected at the expense of the abbey. The tradition is not a fanciful one. Many abbeys possessed town houses staffed by two or three monks, from which their local estates could be administered or from which business could be transacted by the abbot or his officers, and this house probably came into such a category."* Combermere Abbey owned St Mary's Acton and St Mary's Nantwich, and this site would sit between both churches.

\* \* \* \* \* \* \*

We must also point out that 'Namptwich Priory' isn't recorded in the chantry chapels and lands of Cheshire, at the time of the

Dissolution.[91] This most likely means that it had been lost to time, before the mid to late 16th century, when St Lawrence's Chapel and Hospital and St Nicholas' Chapel and Hospital are still recorded.

However its coat of arms remained part of the history of Nantwich, so it must have been important enough for its detail to remain, even if it was a much earlier establishment, and like Joseph Partridge in his history of 1774, told us that it was an ancient tradition that a Priory had existed on Welsh Row near to St Lawrence's Hospital and Chapel.

\* \* \* \* \* \* \*

On the **'Ordnance Survey Town Plan of Nantwich, dated 1876'**, the surveyors have marked the 'Supposed Site of Priory' to the immediate west of the Cheshire Cat (26-36 Welsh Row) and 'Supposed Site of St Lawrence's Hospital' opposite on the other side of the road. The reason they have placed them here mistakenly, rather than at the head of Welsh Row, is because they have mixed up the Wilbraham Almshouses at the head of Welsh Row with the Widow's Almshouses which were located here, but also founded by the Wilbraham Family, and also known as the Wilbraham Almshouses, and now known as the Cheshire Cat.

\* \* \* \* \* \* \*

This Priory or monastic cell is thought by some to have been linked with Combermere Abbey, which was founded in the 1130s by Hugh Malbank, second Baron of Nantwich, as a Savigniac and later Cistercian monastery. This seems possible given the similar coat of arms and their staffs, recorded in the historic records. Combermere Abbey was situated to the south-west of the town of Nantwich, near Whitchurch in Shropshire, and near to Newhall Tower / Castle. The Abbey was dedicated to the Virgin Mary and St Michael.

It is interesting to note that Combermere Abbey was linked with St Mary's Church in Acton, but also St Mary's Church in Nantwich, which are also dedicated to the Virgin Mary, and all three are often stated as being of the 'Blessed Mary'.

Interestingly as well is that Combermere Abbey was linked with and had appropriated: Baddiley Church (to the north-east, between Nantwich and Wrenbury); Church Coppenhall Church (further to the north-east, and now in the town of Crewe); and Child's Ercall Church (to the south, between Market Drayton and Newport in Shropshire); as well as others. These three medieval benefices were also dedicated, like the Abbey, to St Michael. Marbury was also dedicated to St Michael, which is just to the north-west of the Abbey, and was also a medieval benefice.

* * * * * * *

With St Lawrence's Hospital and Chapel, and the Priory (another Hospital?) being located opposite or on or near the site of the Wilbraham's Almshouses, respectively, makes matters even worse when we remember that the Almshouses, were also located at the head of Welsh Row, and were sometimes known as 'Wilbraham's Hospital', as well as older almshouses also being known as 'the Hospitall', see below for further details.

It also didn't help previous researchers and historians that Joseph Partridge was misquoted in many historic and now modern histories, as saying that the hospital for lepers, i.e. St Lawrence's Hospital was situated on or near the site of a Malthouse, when in fact he actually said it was the 'Priory' which was situated there; i.e. *"There is an ancient tradition which holds that **the priory was built upon the site, upon a part of which, now stands the Malt House** occupied by Mr. Bayley, very near the said Alms Houses"* (**'An Historical Account of the Town and Parish of Nantwich, Joseph Partridge, 1774, Pages 8-9'**).

James Hall misquoted him in his history of 1883, by saying that [St Lawrence Hospital] *"is termed in several deeds **"Domus Leprosorum"**, and that, **according to tradition of the town, it stood on or near the site of a "Malt-house,"** then (1774) occupied by Mr. James Bayley, (still standing, but now disused) very near the Almshouses at Welsh Row Head. **The same writer [Joseph Partridge] contends for the existence of a Priory in close proximity to the Hospital [of St Lawrence]; but no mention of any such foundation is to be found in any authentic record.**" '**A History of the Town and Parish of**

***Nantwich or Wych-Malbank, Cheshire, James Hall, 1883 (Republished 1972), Page 53'.***

Sadly I think this is the reason for following historical and modern mistakes of where St Lawrence's Hospital and Chapel was thought to have stood, with this misquote causing confusion right up to the modern day. James Hall also mistakenly links St Lawrence's Hospital and Chapel with Combermere Abbey too, when none of the original records actually include that for St Lawrence's, and why he included this, sometimes in brackets is not clear, never mind the saintly dedication not being anything to do with Combermere Abbey either, or the fact that historic records describe St Lawrence's Chapel as a 'Free Chapel'.

Eric Garton in **'Nantwich: Saxon to Puritan, A History of the Hundred of Nantwich, 1050 to 1642, 1972, Page 79'**, tells us that *"the Hospitals of St. Lawrence and St. Nicholas as they were not under monastic rule."*

Andrew Lamberton believed that 'Malthouse Cottage' or 112-116 Welsh Row, which stood as three, four, five, and six cottages in times past, and which still exists as a timber-framed but much altered single residence, may possibly date back to the 13$^{th}$ century, and was possibly part of either a priory or the Hospital of St Lawrence. According to Historic England (was English Heritage) this building likely dates to the 16$^{th}$ century, although it could be earlier. (**'A Dabber's Nantwich Website: Cottage may be on the site of a 13$^{th}$ century priory or hospital, Andrew Lamberton'** (https://www.dabbersnantwich.me.uk/oldpix23.htm).

Andrew Lamberton and Robin Gray in **'Lost Houses in Nantwich, 2005, Page 12'**, said that St Lawrence's Hospital, or at least part of its complex (or even the supposed priory opposite, see later) *"was still standing in 1653 because it is mentioned in an agreement in the Wilbraham manuscripts. [where] It says that: 'Whereas the said John Thrush being lawfully possessed of a messuage called the Hospitall now divided into three dwellings in/near the Welsh Row in Wich Malbanke and one pasture/croft called the Hospitall croft in Wich Malbanke etc.'"*

The *"messuage called the Hospitall"*, may be misleading, because in historic records 'almshouses' are often known as 'hospitals'.

However it may refer to the Priory, as the early histories of Nantwich, by Partridge and Platt, allude to, and which may in fact, from these historic details and the form of the coat of arms, may have actually been another medieval Nantwich hospital.

In historic directories for Cheshire, for example, **'Kelly's Directory of Cheshire, 1928, Page 291'** under the details for the town of Nantwich, we find that *"Mrs. Ermine Delves, by deed, dated September 5$^{th}$, 1722, gave several houses in Barker street, and two houses and a barn in Love lane, for the purpose of erecting and endowing* **an hospital for poor men** *(natives of Nantwich) and their wives, respectively of the age of fifty years or upwards, to be governed by the same rules and orders as* **Sir Edmund Wright's hospital***, except as to the name and kindred of Wright."*

This, therefore, shows us that 'almshouses' were also known as 'hospitals', and hence, the hospital referred to in the Wilbraham manuscripts which supposedly refers to St Lawrence's Hospital, as *"a messuage called the Hospitall"* and *"one pasture/croft called the Hospitall croft in Wich Malbanke"* may actually refer to earlier almshouses before those known as the Wilbraham Almshouses were built in 1613. It is also interesting that it includes that the messuage was called the 'Hospitall', and in the 1653 deed as being divided into three dwellings.

Again 'almshouses' being referred to as 'hospitals' or 'hospital houses', appears in an Estate Account Book of Thomas Wilbraham, which records the **rents for hospital houses**, 1842-58.[92]

If you consult the section on Hospitals or Almshouses, in Joseph Partridge's History, and James Hall's History, it becomes even more apparent, that 'almshouses' were also known as 'hospitals', with these histories dating from both the late 18$^{th}$ and late 19$^{th}$ centuries. This has obviously caused much confusion, especially if there are a lot of them. Some medieval hospitals were practically early almshouses anyway, there wasn't that much difference.

This is even more apparent when we look at the foundation deed and other deeds for Wilbraham's Almshouses, which actually refer to them as 'Wilbraham's Hospital', and were founded for six poor men, and built in 1613.[93] They are also recorded as having been built in brick and stone, and most likely were in the same form as the two remaining brick and stone derelict almshouses in St Mary's Churchyard at nearby Acton, which were also founded in 1613 by Roger Wilbraham.

***The Two Almshouses at Acton, built in 1613 by Roger Wilbraham***

The foundation deed appears in the Wilbraham Manuscripts at Cheshire Archives and Local Studies (CALS Ref: DTW/A/6), dated 1 February 1613, and is titled on its reverse side as *"Sir Roger Wilbraham's Endowment of his Hospitall in Namptwich."* Attached to the foundation deed are the rules of the Almshouse or Hospital as follows:-

> *"Orders appointed by Sir Roger Wilbraham knight (founder of / an Hospital at Nantwiche) to be observed for ever.*
>
> *This Hospital standing upon the Edge of two parishes viz [namely] Nantwiche / where he was borne, and Acton parishe, where his Grandfather descended.*
>
> *Fforsee, of the Six Almesmen, shalbe of Nantwiche and the two other of / Acton parishe, And if one parishe faile of men capable, the other to supply / that defecte.*

*None shalbe admitted to the Hospitall before he accomplishe the age of / fyfty fyve yeres and have dwelled in the parishe fyve yeres next before his admittance.*

*In the Ellection, a Souldier that hath ventured for the defence & Service / of his Countrie, shalbe preferred before any other person, especially having / served in Ireland, where the founder was Solicitor & Attorney to Queene / Elizabeth some tene yeres, and escaped by God's providence many dangers / by Sea and Land.*

*Ffoure maurkes yerelie wages for dyett, and one maurke, for a blewe or blacke / gowne, to be yerelie allowed to eche Almesman.*

*Out of the Surplusage, above Twenty four poundes per annum in this / dede mentioned, the heires & assignes of the founder, that shall have the / placing of the men, shall cause the Hospitall to be repayred for ever.*

*The Almesmen (as brethren) shall every Sonday at least, repayre together / to their parishe Churche, or to Acton Churche, And for every wilfull / default, certifyed by the Curate, or two Churchwardens, every one shall / forfeite twelve pence to be abated of their stipend and to be distributed / amongste the other brethren.*

*Every one detected, for a notorious blasphemer or drunckard, or infamous for any other detestable Cryme, And likewise any Leper / that may infecte his brethren, shalbe removed by the feoffees in this / dede annexed named their heires & assignes or any two of them; with / the consent of any that shall have the placing of the Almesmen, wittnes / hearunto the hand & seale of the said founder the day & yere first mentioned in / the said Deeds annexed of Indowment. [signed] Roger Wilbraham."*

These deeds which refer to 'Wilbraham's Hospital' (CALS Ref: DTW/A) also tell us that *"augmented the afo[resai]d Hospital with a Field of eight Acres of Land and ap[p]u[rtenances] [hereditary parts] in Henhull, called The Alms-house Meadow, rented for £12 p[er] Ann[um] & distributed among 6 poor people share & share alike."* This therefore also tells us that there was a large field that helped raise money for the Hospital (the 6 Almshouses), and their inhabitants, on the same side of the road, and in Henhull. The deeds also include that £20 per annum was raised for the almsmen from the walling (boiling) of salt.[94]

'Alms house Meadow' is shown on the c1840 Tithe Map of Henhull (CALS Ref: EDT 198/2) as Plot 81, which existed to the immediate north-west of Nantwich Marina, and was then owned by John Tollemache.

Sir Edmund Wright's 1638 Almshouses, which originally stood on the other side of the town, near to the site of St Nicholas' Hospital and Chapel, at the east end of Hospital Street (now on Beam Street), also had a field next to them, called 'Almshouse Meadow', which is shown on Joseph Fenna's 1794 Map of Nantwich.

Also according to a deed dated 29 April 1612 (CALS Ref: DWN/2/124), we find on the reverse it described as *"Sir Frincis Newport his / conveyance* **of the Land / whiche the Almshouse standeth***"*, was sold to Sir Roger Wilbraham, knight, from Sir Francis Newporte of Highe Ercoll, knight. This deed also includes that *"Sir Francis Newporte ... hath bargained sold enfeoffed and confirmed ... All that* **parte of one parcel of land comonlie called or knowne by the name of the Hospitall yard** *(as it is now meened out [partitioned/measured out]) situat[e] lying and being in Wiche Malbanke in the county of Chester and now in the tenure or occupation of Raphe Wilbraham of Wiche Malbanke, aforesaid gent, and lyeth on the Eastparte adjoining to the Landes of the Inheritance of the said Sir Francis Newporte and on the West parte to the landes of the heires of Richard Wright late of the Bell in Wiche Malbanke aforesaid deceased* **and on the South parte to the highe way or pavement leading from the said Wiche towardes Acton Churche***, And on the North parte to the landes of the inheritance of the said Sir Francis Newport"*.[95]

This deed verifies that the land known as 'Hospital Yard' was on Welsh Row next to the site of Wilbraham's Almshouses, and owned by Sir Francis Newport of High Ercall. And also that the land to the West, was actually in the holding of Richard Wright of the Bell, who is linked with the later history of St Lawrence's Chapel and Hospital.

However, contained in the Wilbraham manuscripts which refer to *"a messuage called the Hospitall [in Welsh Rowe]"* may refer to earlier almshouses before those known as the Wilbraham Almshouses were built in 1613.

This may be the case because an earlier Wilbraham deed dated to 12 May 1598 (CALS Ref: DWN/2/116), tells us that *"Francis Newporte of Highe Arcoll in the Countie of Salop Esquire, In his deede indented bearinge date the nyneteeneth daie of Maue in the nyne and thirtieth yere of the reigne of our said Soverigne Ladie the Queenes [?] that nowe is: Did demise Leas grannte sett and coferme Lett unto the said Richard Wilbraham one mes[s]uage ten[emen]te or Hospitall in the Wiche [Nantwich] aforsaid, called or knowne by the name of the Hospitall, One cottage in the Wiche aforsaid wherein Rob[er]te Boyer then dwelled, One other cottage in the Wiche aforsaid then in the tenure or occupation of Marryan Cretchley, one pasture or Crofte Lyinge in the said Wiche called the Hospitall Croft, And all that crofte in the Wiche aforsaid called Saincte Anne Crofte al[ia]s Froggegreaves (excepte nyne butts in the weste ende of the same crofte, beinge the narrowe ende thereof wh[ic]h are of the inheritance of the said Rauffe Wilbraham) one whichehouse of twelve Leades with it appurtenances situate Lyinge and beinge in Wiche aforsaid in a certeyne lane there called greate wood streete, And the site or grounde of one other wichehouse of Six Leades Lyinge in pepp[er] streete [on the south side of Welsh Row, not to be confused with Pepper Street in the town, which was originally known as 'Rotten Row'] in Wiche aforsaid, And alsoe all and all man[ner] of howses edifices buildings orchards gardens yards backside wood commens bryne walling makinge of salte tithes p[ro]fitts comodities and [?] whatsoever with all and singular theire appurtenances unto the said mes[s]uage Hospitall Cotages wichehouses"*.[96]

This historic deed dates to 1598 and quotes an earlier deed of 19 May 1597 (CALS Ref: DWN/2/114), of the transfer of a messuage or property known as the 'Hospitall', from Francis Newport of High Ercall, to Richard Wilbraham, for him and the lives of Rauffe, Roger and Thomas Wilbraham.[97]

The deed referring to the 'Hospitall', also includes lands that were once held by St Nicholas' Hospital, i.e. the Hospitall Croft and

Saincte Anne Crofte alias Froggegreaves. This may be the reason that this property also referred to as a hospital, has been historically attributed wrongly to St Nicholas', on the other side of town.

The inclusion of "*all that crofte in the Wiche aforsaid called Saincte Anne Crofte al[ia]s Froggegreaves (excepte nyne butts in the weste ende of the same crofte, beinge the narrowe ende thereof wh[ic]h are of the inheritance of the said Rauffe Wilbraham)*", also tells us that this property wasn't part of St Lawrence's Hospital, because as we discussed on **'Page 97'** (see above), *"le nine Buttes"*, in a 1548 deed, which is excluded here, was actually part of St Lawrence's, and hence why it was excluded from this holding.

Another deed dated 1608/9 refers to the same property, confirming the agreement.[98]

If we remember that Francis Newport in 1612 sold the land known as the 'Hospital Yard' to Raphe Wilbraham to build his Hospital or Almshouses on, and that the 1612 deed included that "*lyeth on the Eastparte adjoining to the Landes of the Inheritance of the said Sir Francis Newporte*" where Malthouse Cottage exists, had according to the 1597 and 1598 deeds, a messuage or property known as the 'Hospitall' on, then this therefore, confirms that there were earlier almshouses or the remnants of a hospital, existing next and to the east, of the later 1613 Wilbraham's Hospital or Almshouses, and that Malthouse Cottage was this property.

This, therefore confirms "*that the messuage called the Hospitall, now devided into three dwellings, situate in or neere the Welsh Rowe in Wich Malbanke*", in a deed dated 20 August 1653 (CALS Ref: DWN/2/154),[99] confirms that the property known as the 'Hospitall' in 1597, 1598, and 1626 (CALS Ref: DWN/2/131),[100] was almshouses or a hospital, or both in its history, and now survives as Malthouse Cottage, which even in the Victorian and early 20th century consisted of a number of cottages.

This therefore most likely tells us that it was another group of Almshouses, and not part of St Lawrence's Hospital, but could still be on the site of the Priory, which may have been another hospital.

However we know that the Priory isn't recorded in the list of dissolved properties in Cheshire in 1588 and 1590,[101] for it to be the same property referred to as the 'Hospitall' in 1597, and deeds of Francis Newport of High Ercall who held that property do not record it as such, so this later hospital is more likely almshouses, built upon its site as Joseph Partridge told us in his 1774 town history.

It also confirms that Historic England's Listing for Malthouse Cottage is most likely correct and that this building is of a 16th century date, and existed at least as far back as 1597.

This would mean that this property most likely once formed the oldest almshouses in Nantwich, dating as far back if not further than 1597, and that they were originally the property of Sir Francis Newport of High Ercall in Shropshire, but leased by Richard Wilbraham of Nantwich.

It also tells us that the property was most likely utilised as almshouses being known as 'the Hospitall', under the Wilbraham family from at least 1597 until at least 1653, when it was recorded as being divided into three cottages.

It seems likely they were almshouses due to the fact that Wilbraham's Almshouses were then built next door, in 1613. This too may indicate that a priory or medieval hospital was sited here, and hence the location had a long history of accommodating the poor, sick, and needy.

Malthouse Cottage is also known as 112-116 Welsh Row. We are lucky that this historic building still survives, because in the mid to late 1960s the row of cottages was earmarked for demolition, and their plight appeared in the local newspapers.

Malthouse Cottage being 16th century almshouses, also known as 'the Hospital', as well as the 1613 Wilbraham's Almshouses also known as 'Wilbraham's Hospital', and most likely all once forming part of one Hospital complex of almshouses, has made the identification of the site of the two religious establishments known as the Priory and St Lawrence's Hospital & Chapel, much more difficult in the past.

*Old Photograph of Malthouse Cottage*

*Modern Photograph of Malthouse Cottage*

\* \* \* \* \* \* \*

Sir Roger Wilbraham also built a Hospital which was six almshouses for elderly housekeepers, in the mid 1610s, in Monken Hadley, in Greater London. His burial monument and memorial brasses still exist in the local church. Sir Roger lived here as his country residence but was born in Nantwich. He also lived in St John's Gate of the Priory of St John of Jerusalem (the Knights Hospitaller), at Clerkenwell in London. This second residence was given to him by James I.

In Sir Roger Wilbraham's Will, dated 12 November 1616 (National Archives Ref: PROB 11/128/493), he tells us that he leaves to his heirs *"the foundations and endowments of my two pore Hospitalls (called Wilbraham's Hospitalls) one erected at the Nantwiche my Birth place and the other at Hadley in Midd[lesex] beinge my usuall Countrey Dwellinge parishe."*

\* \* \* \* \* \* \*

Interestingly to this study, a descendant of Sir Francis Newport, mentioned in the 1597, 1598, and 1612/13 Nantwich deeds for the property to the east of Wilbraham's Hospital, also known as the 'Hospitall'; who was also called Francis; had founded in 1694, almshouses in their home Shropshire village of High Ercall, which was also known as 'a hospital', for the accommodation of six elderly people.

Interestingly, their local church in High Ercall, next to their large manor house, was dedicated to St Michael, as Child's Ercall in Shropshire also was, whose benefice was owned by Combermere Abbey, which was dedicated to the Blessed Mary and St Michael.

Could this therefore, suggest that the ancestors of Sir Francis Newport had somehow come into possession of a priory or another medieval hospital, on Welsh Row in Nantwich, which was originally owned by Combermere Abbey, and they had replaced the priory or this hospital with almshouses, which were or became known as the 'Hospitall'?

\* \* \* \* \* \* \*

There was also *"a Field of eight Acres of Land and ap[p]u[rtenances] in Henhull, called The Alms-house Meadow"*, being utilised to augment the lives of six almsmen of Wilbraham's 1613 Hospital,¹⁰² see details above, we are also told in a later 23 December 1671 deed *"concerning lands given to Roger Wilbraham's Hospitall at Namptwich, by the Lady Elizabeth Wilbram, Widow"*, that she *"for the settling a better maintenance and livelihood upon the Almsmen being and to be in the Almshouse situate at the end of a certaine street in Wich Malbanke aforesaid called the Welsh Rowe and by way of Addition unto and, Augmentation of the endowment of the same Alsmhouse in such manner as is herein hereafter directed, and for divers other good causes and valuable considerations her thereunto moving hath granted released and confirmed and, by these presents doth grante Release and Confirme unto the said Sir Thomas Wilbraham & Thomas Delves, Raph Wilbraham, Roger Wilbraham, John Crew and Peter Wilbraham, All that Pasture croft or parcel of Land, now divided into Two parts with a Barne situate upon one of the same parts Lying and being in Henhull alias Hendhull in the said County of Chester commonly called or knowne by the name of the little Alflatter or the little Henhull Wood, now or late in the holding of one Thomas Parker or his Tenants and Adjoyning to the Lands of Robert Parker gent, upon the South part to the Lands of the Right Honorable Robert Viscount Cholmundeley upon the North and East parts to the Lands of Sir Robert Cotton, knight, upon the West part."*

This, therefore tells us that a field known as the Alflatter or the little Henhull Wood, which was divided into two, and had a Barne upon it, all of which were in Henhull, was given over to Wilbraham's Almshouses and for the better living of their almsmen.

If we look at the 1840 Henhull Tithe Map (CALS Ref: EDT 198/2) we find that to the immediate north-west of the original six 1613 Wilbraham's Almshouses, where Malbank School now stands, there was in fact a wood and a barn still existent in 1840. Because: Plot 121 in Henhull is named 'Horse Coppice and Barn', owned by George Wilbraham; and Plot 122 is named 'Far Horse Coppice and Road' owned again by George Wilbraham; and by Welsh Row, Plot 78 is named 'Wall Croft' and owned by [the] Nantwich Poor; Plot 79 is named 'Garden' and owned again by

[the] Nantwich Poor; and Plot 80 is named 'Garden' and owned again by [the] Nantwich Poor.

A 'coppice' is a type of wood, and Wall Croft relates to the act of walling or salt boiling, as well as the barn mentioned must be what the 1671 deed relates to, some 170 years later.

\* \* \* \* \* \* \*

Also, according to four historic deeds which are linked with the Almshouses now known as Malthouse Cottage, include: **"one pasture/croft called the Hospitall croft in Wich Malbanke"**, and in two of the deeds, **"another pasture/croft there called Saincte Anne Crofte alias Froggreaves"**, existed.[103 & 104]

Saint Ann's Croft was also known as the Hospital Croft, as revealed in two deeds dated 1 June 1555 (CALS Ref: DWN/2/85), and 3 June 1555 (CALS Ref: DWN/1/40) where we find it states *"one pasture lying in the parishe of Acton called Seint Anne's croft or Hospitall croft."*[105] Also, according to another historic deed (CALS Ref: DWN/2/155) dated 7 April 1654,[106] St Anne's Croft or Hospital Croft was owned by the Hospital of St Nicholas, on the other side of the town, rather than it being anything to do with the Priory, or the Hospital of St Lawrence, albeit near to the latter.

Before the Hospital of St Nicholas owned this field, it must have been annexed to the medieval St Anne's Chapel, situated in the past near the bridge across the Weaver, at the other end of Welsh Row, in order to raise money for the upkeep of the Chapel, and hence the field's original name.

St Anne's Chapel was used by people crossing the River Weaver, originally via a ford, which sometimes meant in times of flood, which were much more frequent in the past, also afforded the people of Welsh Row to attend church, when the passage to St Mary's was impossible and dangerous.

It was licenced for divine services by the Bishop of Lichfield on the 5th January 1389/90, but would have most likely served travellers long before this, praying for a safe crossing.

The Chapel was not recorded in the chantry records at the time of the Dissolution of the Monasteries, so it must have become obsolete before the mid 16th century, and its use most likely waned over the centuries, due to the building of a bridge enabling safe passage.

A bridge of stone over the Weaver was first constructed in 1663, but a timber bridge had existed long before.

* * * * * * *

Wilbraham's Almshouses or Hospital, six cottages built of brick and stone in 1613, later became the responsibility of the Tollemache family in 1692. In 1870, the current houses known as the Tollemache Almshouses (118-128 Welsh Row), were built, which stand further back from the road, than their predecessors, whose site was by the road and in their front gardens.

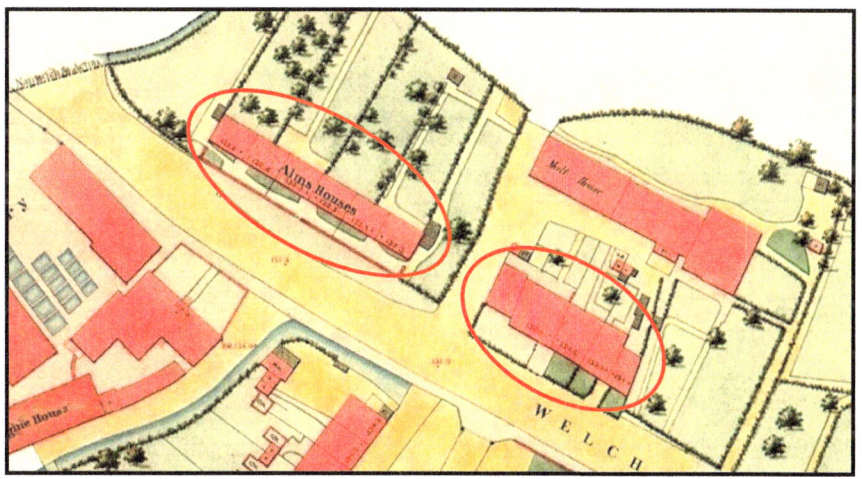

*Wilbraham's Six 1613 Almshouses (Left) and the Earlier Almshouses in front of the Malthouse (Right)*
*Extract from the Board of Health Town Plan: Nantwich, 1851*

*The Tollemache Almshouses on the site of the
1613 Wilbraham's Almshouses or Hospital
(Welsh Row Head, Nantwich)*

\* \* \* \* \* \* \*

It is interesting that in the area of St Lawrence's Chapel and Hospital at Welsh Row Head (as well as that of the Priory), almshouses and a tannery were later built, just like the area where St Nicholas Chapel and Hospital stood, on the other side of the town, at the beginning of Hospital Street, where Sir Edmund Wright's Almshouses were built in 1638, and where a tannery also stood. As we saw above in the first chapter, both tannery sites were near to old watercourses.

\* \* \* \* \* \* \*

The 'Order of Saint Lazarus of Jerusalem', or the 'Leper Brothers of Jerusalem', or the 'Lazarists', was another medieval religious military order, founded by the Crusaders in around 1119. They too are sometimes linked with St Lawrence, and members possibly may have been associated with the 'Lazar House of St Lawrence' in Nantwich.

The plight of people with leprosy was made more widely known because of the suffering of the Crusader King, or King of

Jerusalem, King Baldwin IV. He had suffered from the disease since childhood and was king of Jerusalem from 1174 to 1185. He was buried in the Church of the Holy Sepulchre in the city.

\* \* \* \* \* \* \*

St Lawrence or Laurence is associated with the crippled, the blind, and those suffering from illness, because he is said to have declared that these people were the 'true treasures of the Church', and he identified with the downtrodden and the poor of society. He was also a popular saintly dedication for leper houses.

He was born on 31 December 225AD, possibly in Spain, and cruelly martyred on 10 August 258, in Rome, during the persecution of Christians. His feast day is the same day of his martyrdom. His main shrine is at the Basilica di San Lorenzo fuori le Mura (St Laurence Outside the Walls) in the city of Rome. He is the third most important saint in the holy city, after St Peter and St Paul.

\* \* \* \* \* \* \*

St Lawrence was also the dedication of other medieval hospitals in the UK. Those include:-

- Canterbury, Kent (for leprous monks, built during the reign of Stephen, founded in 1137, by Abbot Hugh, of St Augustine's Abbey);
- Hungerford, Berkshire (hospital for lepers, first recorded in 1228);
- Buckingham, Buckinghamshire (hospital for lepers, first recorded in 1252);
- Warwick, Warwickshire (hospital for lepers, first recorded in 1255);
- Chippenham, Wiltshire (first recorded in 1338);
- Cirencester, Gloucestershire (hospital for lepers, first recorded in the 13$^{th}$ century, and founded by Edith Bisset and the Abbey is patron);
- Bristol (a leper hospital founded by King John when Earl of Montain, in 1208);
- Bodmin (Pontaboye), Cornwall (hospital for lepers, first recorded in 1302);
- Crediton, Devon (first recorded in 1242 and the Bishop of the Manor was patron);

- Hardwick Dam, Setchey Parva, South Lynn, Norfolk (a leper house, in use in 1318);
- Ickburgh, Breckland, Norfolk (St Mary's and St Lawrence's Chapel; a leper hospital or hermitage, founded 1325 by W. Barentun);
- and Appleby, Cumbria (For lepers, founded on the outskirts of Appleby, before 1235).

(**Main Source:** *'The Medieval Hospitals of England, Rotha Mary Clay, 1909'*).

\* \* \* \* \* \* \*

St Lawrence's Chapel and Hospital, and the Priory, and the information about their foundations may infer that because the first Baron of Nantwich, William Malbank founded the Hospital of St Nicholas, and then the second Baron of Nantwich, Hugh Malbank founded Combermere Abbey, then the third Baron of Nantwich, William, may have also founded a religious establishment, either or both, the Hospital of St Lawrence, and the Priory, the latter presumably under the control of the Abbey of Combermere, or another religious order. We know that the third Baron William confirmed his father Hugh's grant of property and lands to Combermere Abbey, by adding further land grants to them, so it seems rather fitting that he may too have founded one or two religious establishments, which were opposite each other at the western end of Welsh Row.

This *"possibility [is] supported by the fact that the advowson [the right to appoint a clergyman to a vacant benefice] of the hospital chapel [of St Lawrence] was partly owned by the barony [of Nantwich, and its lords]"*, which is suggested in **'Monastic and Collegiate Cheshire, Roland W. Morant, 1996, Page 183.'**

\* \* \* \* \* \* \*

If we take into account that according to the town histories of Partridge in 1774, and Platt in 1818, and theirs and later histories: the Priory was likely on the opposite side of Welsh Row to that of the Hospital of St Lawrence; and that they were both sited near to the Almshouses of the Wilbrahams and later the Tollemaches, as well as the once existing Malthouse, at the head of Welsh Row; as well as the Priory, possibly linked with Combermere Abbey or another religious order, on the north of Welsh Row; then we can verify both medieval establishments most likely locations.

It is also interesting to note that on this 1851 Board of Health Town Plan Extract (and the later Ordnance Survey 1876 Town Plan); we find that the old timber-framed row of cottages, which was thought to be part of a religious establishment, and now known as 'Malthouse Cottage', is located nearly opposite, a line of properties, which do not sit parallel to the road, like all the other properties along Welsh Row, which are in line with the street.

This is certainly indicative of these properties following an earlier pattern and form of something more historic than these homes, most likely the plan of St Lawrence's Hospital and Chapel complex; and hence the awkward nature of these properties, dog-legging outwards at an angle from the line of Welsh Row, and directly opposite the site of the Priory.

Local residents as well as map evidence also confirm that there are no drains which would necessitate this deviation from being parallel to the road. The Frogge Brook, which ran from Dorfold Park, past the site of Frogge Mill (located immediately to the west) where the Tannery existed at the head of Welsh Row, and where the brook now runs into a culvert, which may still be seen up a driveway beside 165 Welsh Row.

Here the Frogg Channel or Welsh Row Channel was culverted into an underground brick drain in 1865-6, with the plans designed by George Latham, a Nantwich Architect. This underground culvert, which replaced the open-to-the-street channel, runs along Welsh Row to Second Wood Street, and then into the River Weaver. In the past Welsh Row was even known as 'Frog Row' and the 'Frog-channel' ran down its middle. The culvert and much of its water was later diverted to another brook in the 1980s, by Malbank School, after the Weaver and Frogge Brook flooded Welsh Row in the 1960s and 1970s.

According to the **'Crewe Chronicle, 15 February 1973, Page 17'**, Metallic Roadways, a Hanley (Stoke on Trent) firm, were awarded the contract for the Welsh Row flood relief scheme, which was to go ahead forthwith.

There was also an old footpath which would have been another historic driveway to Dorfold Hall, which began to the rear of the Old Tannery at the head of Welsh Row, and began from the driveway which still exists to the immediate south-east of 165 Welsh Row. This old lane passed the original site of the medieval 'Frogge Mill' which existed to the rear of the Old Tannery. Its Mill Pond can be seen on the 1851 and 1875-6 Maps of Nantwich. This lane or footpath is shown as the 'Dorfold Footway' on Joseph Fenna's 1794 Map of Nantwich. However, this begins further from the odd building alignment to the east, so would have had no bearing on its historic orientation.

A well on the south side of Welsh Row, next to the odd building alignment where the houses don't sit parallel to the road, may record the location of St Lawrence's Well, with a 'P' for a water pump on the old Ordnance Survey maps, which most likely indicates a well, existing to the south side of Welsh Row.

On the Ordnance Survey's Six Inch to the Mile 1899 Map this 'P' for a water pump is the only one of two shown on Welsh Row which marks out its importance. The other is shown to the north-west next to the old Tannery.

According to a local resident, in a front lounge of a property on the south side of Welsh Row, where the properties dog leg from the road, hidden below the floorboards of a ground floor room, exists, a four to five-foot diameter well. This could actually be a better candidate for the holy well known as St Lawrence's Well, than that across the road, which used to exist to provide water for the Malthouse and kiln. St Lawrence's Well was used to treat the people suffering from leprosy, housed at the hospital.

Cleanliness and washing in healing water were thought at the time to be an important part of leprosy treatment. It is also interesting that in the historic past, when this house was built, the well wasn't removed (albeit believed to have been capped in modern times), and was instead retained inside the house, which you wouldn't think was standard practice, unless it was significant, in a historic or even religious standpoint.

The water pump shown on historic mapping sits just to the immediate south-east of this property, and both the encapsulated well and pump may have been fed from the same water source.

The Hospital, Priory, and Well's most likely locations have been suggested on the 1851 Board of Health Map on the next page.

The Maltkiln or Malthouse and its associated well, as all malt houses had a large well to utilise for the brewing of beer, may have been the well which Nantwich Priory also used, and the later almshouses.

It is very very unlikely that St Lawrence's Well, which was used for and by the lepers, would have been utilised by any other properties, and certainly not for the production of beer, due to the fear of contracting leprosy, by the surrounding medieval townsfolk. We only have to remember the recent fear of contracting Covid in our modern age, and the use of masks and handwash. Leprosy would have been feared much more in earlier times than even the recent pandemic.

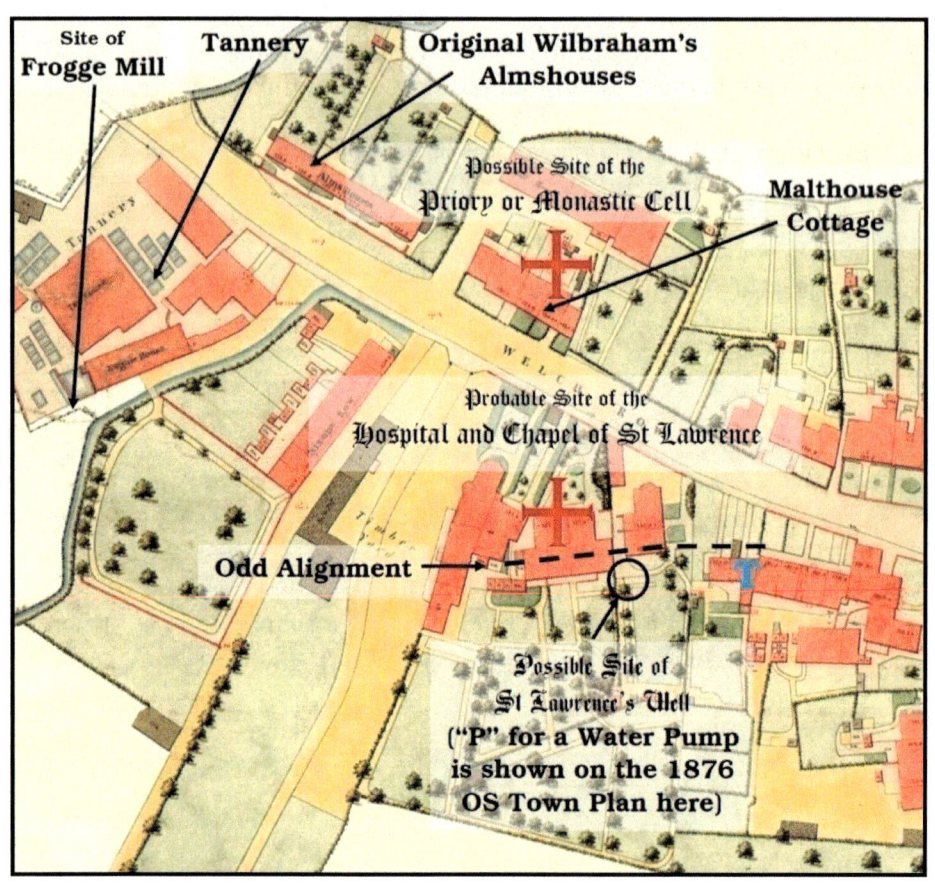

*Possible Locations of the Priory or Monastic Cell and the Hospital and Chapel of St Lawrence and St Lawrence's Well, Extract from the Board of Health Town Plan: Nantwich, 1851*

A three-storey painted white old brick terraced house, at the blue 'T' on the map, to the left, is all that is left of a large tall homestead, which is thought to have been originally timber-framed, and the tall pitched roof, and purlins jutting out of the side brickwork gable walls, prove that it was once thatched; then the odd alignment which begins with this building, to the east; tells us that whatever stood at this dog-leg angle, travelling west; was older than the late 16$^{th}$ or early 17$^{th}$ century, that parts of this house must date from.

This would be a perfect fit for the redevelopment of a possible religious hospital and chapel complex, straight after its removal at the end of the Dissolution.

This tall three-storey painted white house, which is all that is remains of a longer homestead, is known as 141 Welsh Row, and is a Grade II listed building.

***All that remains of 141 Welsh Row***
***(The tall painted white house on the left)***

Two historic cottages also existed between: 'Laurel Cottage' otherwise known as 143 Welsh Row; and 149 Welsh Row; with one cottage at the front, conjoined to the other at the back, which we are told in a property auction advert in the **'Northwich Guardian, Saturday 19 September 1891, Page 8'**, were *"two brick, timbered, and thatched cottages, being No. 145 and 147"*.

According to **'Nantwich Urban District Council's 1946 Housing Report'**, of which details were kindly provided by Nantwich Historian, Andrew Lamberton, we are told that:-

*"**Nos. 145 and 147.** A pair of old half-timbered cottages – formerly thatched but now roofed with corrugated iron. The beamed ceilings of the living rooms are low, the walls are damp, and one window is fixed. The west bedroom is poorly lighted."*

And:-

*"**No. 147.** The back kitchen is small and low, the walls and ceiling are defective. The lighting of the east bedroom is poor. No sink, pantry, washing boiler, or coal store.*

*These cottages, which are probably of seventeenth century construction, are incapable of being re-conditioned at a reasonable cost to comply with present day standards. Both cottages are owned by an aged couple, who occupy No. 145. They should remain undisturbed during their lifetime; afterwards the cottages should be demolished."*

This therefore also reveals that these lost properties were timber-framed, much like 141 Welsh Row was, and 153 Welsh Row still is. They may have even formed part of the Hospital of St Lawrence's buildings, but much altered, and sadly now mainly lost to time. They are believed to have been demolished in 1960/61.

We must also notice that this odd alignment is in a much more easterly direction than the houses and Malthouse Cottage, on the opposite side of the road, as well as those on the same side of the road which all follow the road's orientation.

Is this indicative of these properties following the form and layout of St Lawrence's Chapel, and possible attached Hospital Hall or Infirmary, which would have faced the rising sun on the feast day of St Lawrence, presumably the 10$^{th}$ of August, as other medieval religious buildings faced the rising sun on their saint's feast day, in the medieval majority?

When comparing the odd alignment of historic buildings at the Head of Welsh Row in Nantwich, Cheshire, where St Lawrence's Hospital and Chapel is thought to have existed; to three historic churches in Shropshire, all dedicated to St Laurence / Lawrence as well; we see that the alignment is very very similar.

These churches in Shropshire dedicated to St Law[/u]rence are: Ludlow; Church Stretton; and Little Wenlock.

Other churches dedicated to St Lawrence in and around Cheshire, are: Over Peover (Cheshire); Biddulph (Staffordshire); Rushton Spencer (Staffordshire); and Eyam (Derbyshire).

Medieval Churches and Chapels were orientated to the sunrise on the Saint's Feast Day of its dedication, in these cases St Lawrence or St Laurence.

Notice how similar the alignment is, within just a few degrees of each other; albeit taking into account the different longitude and latitude of their locations, the dates of construction, and heights above sea level, meaning that there is some slight deviation.

St Lawrence's Church at Little Wenlock is a near-perfect match for the odd alignment of buildings at an angle to Welsh Row. Please see the diagrams below.

This would therefore suggest that this odd building alignment at the Head of Welsh Row, may record St Lawrence's Chapel as being located here, and later historic buildings, recording its form later in history, right to the present day; much like High Street in the centre of Nantwich, records the layout of the moat of the once standing Norman Castle.

(For more on Church Orientation, please see *'Church Orientation, Alignment and Solar Worship; with Examples from Cheshire and North Staffordshire, Charles E. S. Fairey, 2018'*, @ https://www.mysticmasque.com/history-mystery/church-orientation-alignment-and-solar-worship).

It certainly presents further evidence as well as the early histories of Nantwich, that, St Lawrence's was on this side of Welsh Row.

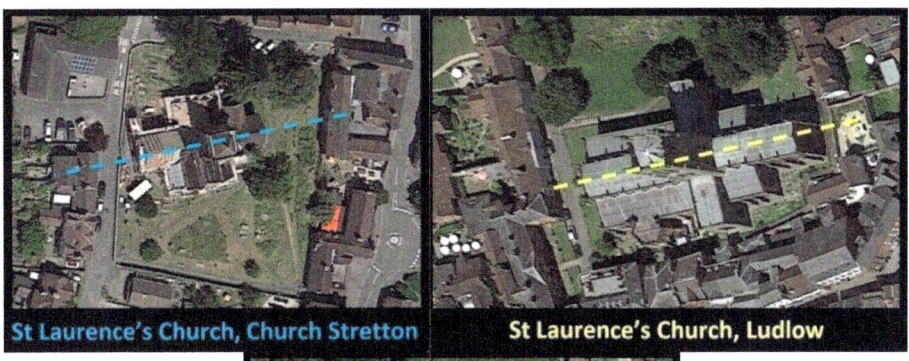

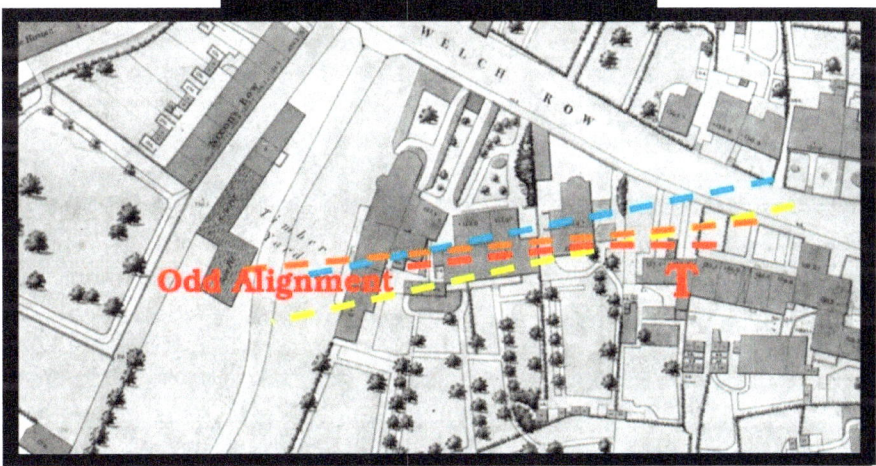

***Comparison of the Odd Building Alignment
at Welsh Row Head, to Three Shropshire
"St La(u/w)rence's" Churches***

*The above images have been reproduced under
Google Maps Satellite Imagery's fair usage policy.
Imagery © 2022 Bluesky, Infotera Ltd & COWI A/S, CNES / Airbus,
Getmapping plc, Infotera Ltd & Bluesky, Maxar Technologies,
Map data © 2022 Google (https://www.google.co.uk/maps)*

\* \* \* \* \* \* \*

Further evidence for St Lawrence's Hospital being located on the south side of Welsh Row (and opposite the site of Nantwich Priory) comes from historic deeds.

In a historic deed dated 6 June 1590, (CALS Ref: DWN/2/105) we are told that *"a parcel of lands and possessions late of Richard Wrighte, in the county of Chester, a croft meddow in Monkes Copenhall called Copenhall Hea, the tithes of Alvaston, one pasture called Roughfeld in Hemhull, the moiety of one croft containing* **one and a half acres called the chappell feld in WicheMalbanke and Acton**, **two acres called chappell crofte** *and one salt house of six leaden fats, the moiety of* **a close called chappell feild**, *and the tithes* **belonging to the late chapel of St. Lawrence**, *amounting in all to the annual value of 77 shillings and 6 pence"*, was leased by Queen Elizabeth, to John Brene, uncle to Margarett and Elizabeth Wrighte, the daughters and heirs of Richard Wrighte, gentleman, deceased. And out of the said grant all advowsons, presentations, woods and underwoods, wards, marriages, etc, an annual rent to the Queen's feodary of Cheshire, of 75 shillings and 6 pence, and to the clerk for valuing the premises, 2 shillings, for the consideration money of £6, 13 shillings and 4 pence.[107]

The inclusion of 'Chappell Field' and 'Chappell Croft', both being linked with St Lawrence's [Chapel], and that they lay in Wiche Malbank [Nantwich] and Acton, and that they were in the hands of the Crown; and come straight after the Grant of 1588 and the Indenture of Sale of 1590, by William and Thomas Kirkham, of Gray's Inn, Gentlemen of Middlesex, we saw above; then the location of these fields further adds weight to the location of the Chapel, and therefore the leper hospital, and later hospital for ill, poor, or infirm people.

Due to St Lawrence's Hospital being linked with Richard Wright, the last recorded chaplain of its Chapel, and that its lands were held by the heirs of him, and not Francis Newport of High Ercall, who owned the property known as the 'Hospitall', opposite, leased to the Wilbraham family, we discussed above, also rules out that they were part of St Lawrence's Hospital, and again reiterates

Malthouse Cottage's use as Almshouses, or as another hospital/priory.

If we look at the Tithe Maps in the locality, i.e.: Nantwich, c1846 (CALS Ref: EDT 285/2); Acton, c1842 (CALS Ref: EDT 1/2; and Henhull, c1840 (CALS Ref: 198/2); we find that the fields on the north side of Welsh Row and the Chester Road, are actually located in Henhull township, and not Acton, but the fields to the south of Welsh Row and Chester Road, and more specifically around the tannery, which stood at the western end of Welsh Row, are actually located in Acton township; also the fields to the east of these, on both sides of Welsh Row, are part of the Township of Nantwich.

This then certainly suggests that this lease dated 6 June 1590, which includes the 'Chappell Field' and 'Chappell Croft', both being linked with St Lawrence's [Chapel], and that they lay in Wiche Malbank [Nantwich] and Acton; that these premises were on the south side of Welsh Row because that area was in Nantwich and Acton townships, rather than the north side of Welsh Row, which was in Nantwich and Henhull townships.

The area of the land of the Chapel Field and Chapel Croft, being in total three and a half acres, could easily fit in the area near the Tannery, right next door and to the immediate west of where the above conjectured location of St Lawrence's Hospital and Chapel existed.

James Hall, in his **'History of Nantwich, 1883, Page 54'**, also tells us that according to the Inquisition Post Mortem of Richard Wright, he died with *"the thythes of the formerly dissolved free Chapel of St. Lawrence"*, and of *"a pasture called Chapel croft, and half of another pasture called the Chapel-field adjacent, lying in Acton."*

Another document, the Will of Randle Wilbraham of Nantwich, Esquire, dated 28 December 1731, details some of his properties, including *"one field called the Frog Pooles in Nantwich and Acton (purchased from Richard Gill, Carrier)"*. This again reiterates that the land on this side of the road, where Frog Pooles was situated, is known to be in Nantwich and Acton.

It is also interesting to note, that according to Joseph Fenna's Map of Nantwich 1794, there is a field known as 'Gill's Meadow', next to 'Near & Great Frog Greaves' and 'St Anne's croft'. This most likely means that in 1731, as the above document tells us, the field known as 'Frog Pooles', was later known as 'Gill's Meadow'.

We have to point out though, that both Henhull and Acton townships were in the parish of St Mary's Church of Acton. But other historic deeds for the north side of Welsh Row, and beyond the township of Nantwich, which are in Henhull Township, usually include that it is in Henhull, and not Acton.

\* \* \* \* \* \* \*

An Assignment of Lease concerning *"part of one pasture in the parish of Acton called **Seint Anne croft or hospitall croft"*,[108] and a Lease concerning *"part of one pasture in the parish of Acton called **Seint Anne croft or hospitall croft"*,[109] both dating to 1555, are also revealing, because Joseph Fenna's 1794 Map of Nantwich, informs us that 'St Anne's Croft' existed next to 'Great & Near Frog Greaves', to the south-west of Welsh Row, and because in the two above historic deeds it is also referred to as 'Hospitall Croft', then this may place St Lawrence's Hospital on the south side of Welsh Row. Also, notice that it is included in Acton, and we know that this side of the old road to Chester was in Acton Township, whereas the fields to the north side were in Henhull Township, as pointed out above. We have to point out though, that St Anne's Croft was sometimes associated with the lands held by St Nicholas' Hospital, so again, it has caused much confusion.

However, another deed, which concerns *"the gift and grant of **one field or pasture called Frogge Polo in Wich Malbank**, lying between land of William Davenport on one side and **land of the Chapel of St. Laurence** and land lately that of Richard Larketon on the other side"* in 1522,[110] is also interesting, and relevant to this study, because we know from above, that 'Frogg Polo' or 'Frog Pooles' was known later as 'Gill's Meadow' on the 1794 Map of Nantwich, and firmly places the land of the Chapel of St Laurence on the south side of Welsh Row, next to the fields known as 'Frog Greaves', 'Frog Polo or Pooles', 'St Anne's Croft or Hospitall Croft'.

This therefore fully proves along with all the other evidence above, where the Hospital and Chapel of St Lawrence was situated, as well as the two fields we discussed above, known as 'Chappell Croft' and 'Chappell Field', which must have been even closer to the site of the Chapel and Hospital.

\* \* \* \* \* \* \*

Eric Garton told us in his **'Nantwich: Saxon to Puritan, Page 69'** that he believed that *"the site of the Hospital of St. Lawrence cannot now be identified but is probably where a fellmonger's business now is in Welsh Row"*. A fellmonger which means a dealer in animal hides or skins, places this site firmly as the Tannery, which used to exist on the south side of Welsh Row Head, opposite the Wilbraham / Tollemache Almshouses, existing behind and beside No. 165 or Tannery House.

Other than Partridge or Platt in their histories of the town, only Eric Garton thought that St Lawrence's was on the south side of Welsh Row, albeit further west to its now proven actual site.

\* \* \* \* \* \* \*

This also means that the possible existence of a Priory (which may have been another medieval hospital) on the opposite side of the road, where the Malthouse was later located, as Joseph Partridge in his 1774 History of Nantwich told us, is most likely true.

The property we discussed above, known as the 'Hospitall', 'Hospitall Croft', and 'Hospitall Yard' either refers to: almshouses existing here from the 16th century, which were later bought by the Wilbraham's; before and after their Wilbraham's Almshouses next door were built in 1613 and to their west; and then rebuilt, and as we still know them as the Tollemache Almshouses; or that the Priory existed as another medieval hospital, serving pilgrims, the poor, and infirm, as its coat of arms indicates, and it was later utilised as the site of three, four, or five successive almshouse dwellings, now known as Malthouse Cottage.

The latter seems more likely, when using the detail Joseph Partridge claimed, as well as the detail in the earlier historic references, and the coat of arms detail.

This means that the accepted history of Nantwich has to be rewritten, and Joseph Partridge reevaluated as one of the great Nantwich's Historians, as well as the acceptance of the actual sites of these two medieval religious establishments.

It is even more evident now that any chance of archaeological evaluations at the Head of Welsh Row, and the investigation of historic buildings in the area, is of paramount importance, going into the future.

\* \* \* \* \* \* \*

The above deed dated 6 June 1590, also tells us that Queen Elizabeth leased the lands to John Brene, uncle to Margarett and Elizabeth Wrighte, the daughters and heirs of Richard Wrighte, gentleman, deceased. This presents further problems with the sites of the Priory and the Hospital of St Lawrence, and created problems for previous researchers, because we also know from another deed, that Richard Wright held land on the other side of the road, in Henhull township, where in the past, since James Hall's 1883 History of Nantwich, the mix up of the site of St Lawrence's began.

In another deed, dated 11 June 1590, the holdings of the Wrights to the north of Welsh Row, are repeated in a Lease that concerns *"a croft in Henhull, lying between the lands of Thomas Chetwood and Thomas Aston on the East, and lands of the heirs of Richard Wright on the West, and the lands of Lawrence Wright on the North, and of the said Thomas Sparke on the South"*.[111]

Another deed this time dated 29 April 1612,[112] (which is related to the deed we discussed a few pages above, of a messuage called 'the hospitall', and 'the hospitall croft', dated 19 May 1597), tells us that a Feoffment by Sir Francis Newporte of Highe Ercoll, Shropshire, Knight, to Sir Roger Wilbraham, Knight, one of the Masters of Requests in Ordinary to the King and Surveyor of H.M.'s Court of Wards and Liveries, of *"a parcel of land called the hospitall yard in WICHE MALBANCKE now in the tenure of Raphe*

*Wilbraham, gentleman, on the East adjoining lands of the inheritance of the said Sir Francis Newporte,* **on the West lands of the heirs of Richard Wright, late of the Bell in Wich Malbancke, deceased**, *on the South the high way or pavement from the said Wiche towards Acton Church, and on the North lands of the inheritance of the said Sir Francis."* Again Richard Wright is referred to, as well as that he was late of the Bell.

Richard Wright was in fact the innkeeper of a large coaching inn, known as 'The Bell' which was located to the south-east of Swine Market, next to the High Street. He was very wealthy, and as we see here also held land, some of which directly relates to our study.

These deeds link Richard Wright to the lands on both sides of the road, and the two religious establishments thought to have existed here. This made the process of locating each even more difficult, recently and in the past.

Richard was also the last Chaplain of St Lawrence's Chapel and was given a pension.

Richard was also granted some rents of the dissolved Abbey of Combermere, along with Thomas Holmes.[113]

Richard Wright's heirs, his daughters, Margaret and Elizabeth, married, but lost their husbands, and after being widows, when they died they gave two silver flagons and a silver plate to the Church of St Mary's (Nantwich), as well as the alms or tithes of the Chapel of St Lawrence.

This seems rather fitting with their father being linked with the final stages of St Lawrence's and St Nicholas' Hospitals, as well as the Guildhall.

We are told in **'Old Cheshire Churches, Raymond Richards, 1947, Pages 248-254'**, that these vessels were:-

> "*Two large silver flagons of 1659 each inscribed "The guift of Eliz. Davenport and Marg[ere]t. Woodnoth, widdowes, To ye church of Namptwich 1659" together with the arms of both families.*"

And a *"Silver paten of the same period given by the same donors."*

\* \* \* \* \* \* \*

The lands and their tithes, of Richard Wright, which were given by his daughters to St Mary's Church of Nantwich, and may have been part of the lands held by St Lawrence's Chapel, maybe: Plot 86, Causeway Field, Plot 87, Tanyard Croft, and Plot 88, Garden; which were all owned by the 'Churchwardens of Nantwich'. These may be seen on Cheshire East's Tithe Map Website @ https://maps.cheshireeast.gov.uk/tithemaps/, and to the immediate south-east of the Canal's Aqueduct at the Head of Welsh Row.

\* \* \* \* \* \* \*

It is also possible that St Lawrence's Chapel and Hospital, when it acted as a 'leper colony', had its own distinct cemetery, and remains of the lepers of Nantwich may still be waiting to be discovered, nevermind its Masters and staff being buried inside the once standing Chapel.

This is the case with the leper Hospital and Chapel of St Giles that stood in Boughton in Chester. The area around it became known as the village of 'Spital', named after the ho***spital*** itself. This cemetery still exists, to the south of the A51 or Christleton Road, at The Mount, in Boughton.

*St Giles Cemetery in Boughton, Chester*

Like St Laurence's was on the outskirts of the town of Nantwich, St Giles' was on the outskirts of the City of Chester, due to the fear of contact and spread of leprosy.

Nearby was also 'Gallows' Hill', a site of an old tree as well as an artificial gallows, for the execution by hanging of criminals. Many gallows sites existed on the outskirts of cities and towns, and on main roads, where justice could be viewed by passersby, and remind them of the cost of criminal acts.

The actual site of the gallows is still marked by the 'Boughton Obelisk' or 'Memorial' to the Protestant Martyr George Marsh, who was burned at the stake here, in April 1555. His ashes were collected by his followers and buried at St Giles Cemetery.

* * * * * * *

* * * * * * *

# The Hospital of the Holy Cross and St George (Wybunbury)

The *'Monastic and Collegiate Cheshire, Roland W. Morant, 1996, Page 184'*, tells us that there was a *"hospital mentioned by Gasquet at Wybunbury, occurring in 1464 and dedicated to St George and the Holy Cross, [and that it] may be identical with a fraternity of the Holy Cross said to have existed at nearby Nantwich [Kettle, 1980, 126]"*.[114]

Roland W. Morant also tells us on Page 191, of the above that:-

*"There is mention of a hermitage at Wybunbury. In a lease of William Heyworth, bishop of Coventry and Lichfield, two gardens were demised to Nicholas Baker the hermit for ninety-nine years, on condition that they were to be held by fit priests or honest hermits. The lease bears the date 1424 [Magna Britannia, Daniel Lysons, 1810, Page 826]".*

This tells us that as well as a medieval hospital, there was also a hermitage in Wybunbury.

Also according to *'Monasticon Anglicanum: A History of the Abbies and Other Monasteries, Hospitals, Frieries, and Cathedral and Collegiate Churches, with Their Dependencies, in England and Wales ... Originally Published in Latin, Volume 8, 1825, Page 756-7'*, we are told that according to Bishop Tanner, at Wybunbury *"was an Hospital of a Master and brethren, dedicated to the Holy Cross and St. George, before A.D. 1464."*

The site of this hospital is recorded in the 1846 Tithe Award of Wybunbury, as 'Hospital Bank' and 'Hospital Bank Garden', as Plots 243 and 244 respectively, and on the accompanying Tithe Map (CALS Ref: EDT 446/2). They are sited to the southern half of the current old graveyard, and to the south of the remaining medieval tower of St Chad's Church.

'Hospital Bank' is also shown in the same area on the Ordnance Survey 1st Edition 25 inch to the mile Map, dating to 1875-6. The related 6-inch-to-the-mile Map can be viewed on Cheshire East's Tithe Map Website @ https://maps.cheshireeast.gov.uk/tithemaps/.

There isn't much relating to this hospital than that revealed above, but it was likely a place for those ill of health, elderly, or desitute, that had lived in the large parish of Wybunbury.

A school also stood in the churchyard, to the north-west.

* * * * * * *

St George or the Holy Cross was the dedication of other medieval hospitals in the UK. Those include:-

- Sittingbourne, Kent (Holy Cross; first mentioned in 1225);
- Colchester, Essex (Holy Cross and St Helen; first recorded 1235, and founded by W. de Lanvalle of St Helen's Gild);
- Reigate, Surrey (St Mary the Virgin and Holy Cross; first recorded before 1240, and founded by W. de Warenne);
- Pevensey, Sussex (Holy Cross; first recorded in 1292);
- Winchelsea, Sussex (Holy Cross, first recorded in 1253);
- Winchester, Hampshire (St Cross; first recorded circa 1136, and founded by Henry de Blois, and the Knights and Bishop were patrons);
- Woodstock (without), Oxfordshire (St Cross; hospital for lepers, first recorded in 1231);
- Stratford on Avon, Warwickshire (Holy Cross; first recorded in 1269, and founded by the Fraternity of the Holy Cross);
- Bath (Holloway or Lyncomb), Somerset (St Cross and St Mary Magdalene; hospital for lepers, first recorded before 1100, and founded by Walter Hosate, and the Priory as patron);
- Shrewsbury, Shropshire (St George, first recorded in 1162);
- Yeovil, Somerset (St George and St Christopher; first recorded in 1477, and founded by J. Wobourne);
- Bodmin, Cornwall (St George; first recorded in 1405);
- and Tavistock, Devon (St George; founded by Tremayne).

(**Main Source: *'The Medieval Hospitals of England, Rotha Mary Clay, 1909'*).**

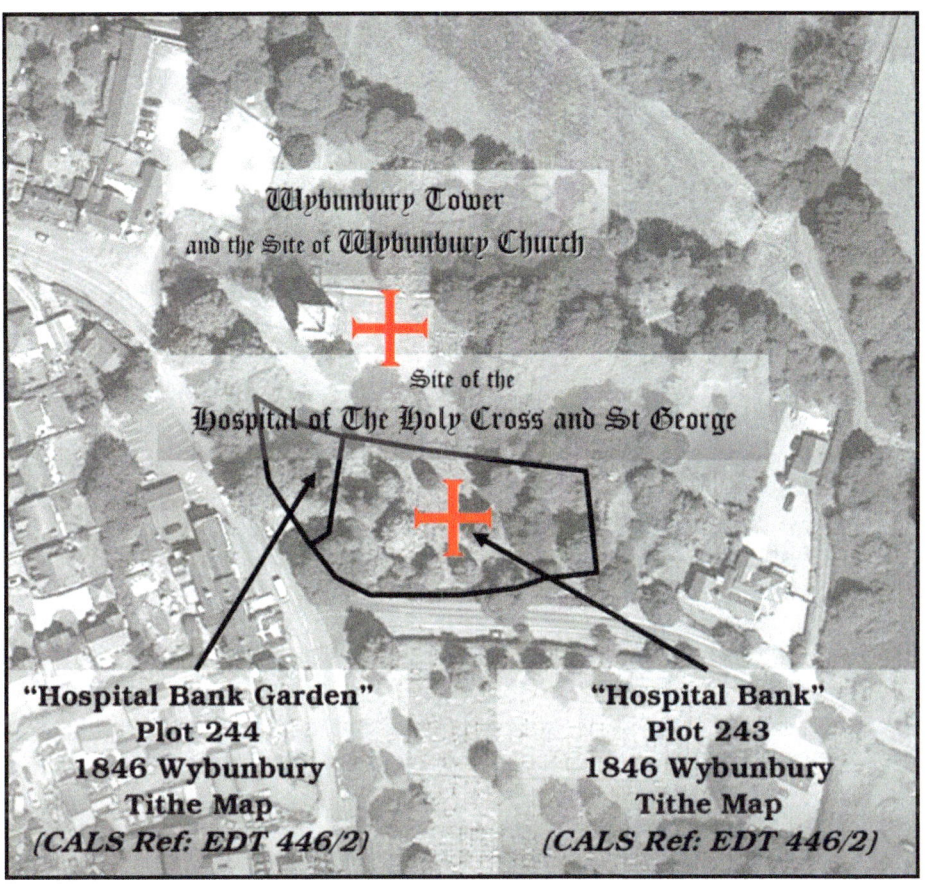

**The Site of The Hospital of the Holy Cross and St George at Wybunbury**

*Google Maps Satellite Imagery has been reproduced under their fair usage policy. Imagery © 2022 Bluesky, Infotera Ltd & COWI A/S, CNES / Airbus, Getmapping plc, Infotera Ltd & Bluesky, Maxar Technologies, Map data ©2022 Google (https://www.google.co.uk/maps)*

\* \* \* \* \* \* \*

St George was the favourite saint of the Crusaders. During the Battle of Mondgisard, where the Crusaders were victorious, it was sworn that the Saracens were driven headlong by the mounted figure of St George. St George himself was thought to be buried nearby at Lydda (now Lod). He gained his chivalric image in later medieval literary works, due to the Crusaders' veneration of him as their preferred military saint.

You can just imagine the Crusaders using a battle cry of *"For the Holy Cross and St George"*, when advancing against the Saracen forces in battles for the Holy Land. The Crusaders were known to carry 'the True Cross' into battle. It was a large cross that reputedly held pieces of the Cross upon which Christ was crucified, inside a small reliquary container within it.

During the First Crusade's battle of Dorylaeum on 1 July 1097, the crusaders strengthened their resolve by repeating *"Stand fast together, trusting in Christ and the Victory of the Holy Cross!"*.[115]

St George was made the Patron Saint of England by King Edward III, around 1350, when he created the Order of the Garter (a chivalric or knightly order), in the saint's name. His feast day is 23 April.

His legend can be a metaphor of a holy warrior wearing the cross, protecting a maiden (the Mother Church), from Satan the Dragon.

With the Guild of the Holy Cross at Nantwich, and the existence of St George's Chapel in the North Transept of St Mary's Church, this gives a good link with the medieval hospital and its dedication at Wybunbury, to both the Guild and Church of Nantwich.

Bishop Tanner's remarks (see above), told us that the hospital was staffed by *"a Master and brethren"*, which certainly sounds like the Brethren of the Guild of the Holy Cross, at Nantwich (see later).

*St George's Chapel, North Transept, St Mary's Church, Nantwich*

\* \* \* \* \* \* \*

The Holy Cross was the cross upon which our Lord, Jesus Christ was crucified, and the church of Acton, is said to have had a relic of the Holy Cross during the medieval period. Please see below for discussion of this.

\* \* \* \* \* \* \*

# Medieval Hospitals

Medieval hospitals were not like hospitals as we know them today. The word came from the Latin 'hospitalis', meaning they gave hospitality to people who were travelling, i.e. those journeying seeking shelter, such as pilgrims.

These hospitals would often only accommodate travellers such as pilgrims and poor wayfarers, for one night only, but sometimes rich travellers used these houses to accommodate their entourage, as we saw was a problem at St Nicholas' Hospital in Nantwich, as well as at Combermere Abbey.

The other kind of medieval hospitals, as we have seen above, were more like almshouses, accommodating the poor, elderly, and destitute. These were also known as 'bedehouses'.

At Nantwich, St Nicholas' Hospital and Nantwich Priory were most likely a combination of the above, as well as housing some sick or injured people.

There were some which also housed and cared for those of ill health, both in a treatment stand-point, but also in a spiritual way too. This is ever-present in the large number of medieval hospitals which housed and cared for sufferers of leprosy, as we saw above with Nantwich's St Lawrence's Hospital.

Leper hospitals were often distinct hospitals as they were segregated from the general populous, with an enclosed complex, much more like a monastery, with many lepers having the illness for life, with no hope of a cure.

Leper hospitals became less necessary as the Middle Ages passed, and many became hospitals or almshouses for the old, infirm, and sick. This was also the case for St Lawrence's, in its later history.

Most hospitals were either founded by monastic houses, or rich benefactors, who showed their charity to their fellows and wider communities.

They were essentially monastic in their running. They were religious establishments, run by the monastic orders, institutions, or religious groups, giving the faithful: shelter, help, and treatment, sometimes health-wise, but usually spiritually.

Often hospitals were located in or near urban settlements, and often on busy routeways. This had the added benefit of passing charity from members of the public, who would often give money or food to the residents.

If the hospitals were located at the edge of settlements, this gave the added opportunity of nearby fields to utilise for the growing of foodstuffs, etc, and/or the establishment of dedicated hospital orchards, gardens, and herb beds. This meant that residents would live both a spiritual and pastoral existence, something thought of as very important in historic times, for both, the health of the spirit and mind, as well as the body.

Each hospital had a master (or warden), who was also usually the chaplain of its chapel. These masters or chaplains were most often appointed by the hospital's benefactor or patron. They administered the running of such establishments, often with a number of brethren, sisters, lay folk, and/or novices helping to run and staff them.

The hospital Master, Warden, or Chaplain, wasn't always found working at their hospital post, and often had other benefices, often deputising their brothers and sisters with the full-time management of each establishment. Often they were also priests officiating at local or sometimes far away hospitals, churches, monasteries, etc. The master was also sometimes known as a 'Prior'.

The staff of medieval hospitals could consist of a number of brothers or sisters, to care for those accommodated, along with lay folk, who ran the day-to-day business of the institute, such as cooking, cleaning, brewing, etc, etc. Some of the lay folk would also be in the business of collecting the hospital's running costs, whether they were in the form of charity, alms, gifts, bequests, rents, tithes, tolls, food, drink, etc etc.

The brothers or brethren of the hospital were also usually chaplains or novices, schooled or being schooled in the divine arts; and the sisters, were usually nuns, who had devoted their lives to the service of the hospital and its patients.

Each patient or resident would be expected to pray to God with the Lord's Prayer, as well as prayers for the Mother of God, the Virgin Mary, and the recital of psalms, throughout the day. They also were expected to give time throughout the day to pray for their travels, monetary woes, elderly nature, or ill health, in the Chapel or Church associated with each hospital.

Residents were also often directed to pray for the founders, patrons, or benefactors of the hospital.

In the hospitals which were more like almshouses, generally had strict rules for accommodation, usually set by the patron, as we saw above with the early $17^{th}$ century Wilbraham's Hospital (Almshouses) on Welsh Row in Nantwich. Sometimes prospective residents had to have financial backers in order to gain entry, or agree to all the rules beforehand and for life.

However, we must remember that the almshouses of the post-medieval era are usually made up of distinct residences, rather than cells or areas of communal living within an infirmary hall, which we find in medieval hospitals.

The chaplain or master of the Hospital, would also carry out the religious services in the chapel, as well as giving Mass to the residents, but also give blessings seeking divine intervention to help those in need.

He of course, especially where hospitals housed the poor, elderly, sick, and injured, would officiate at the time of death of the patients/residents, at their funeral and burial.

In the medieval period, ill health was seen as God-given, i.e. their sins had caused their problems, so prayer and faith were seen as essential to the recovery and treatment of the patient, or at least the saving of one's soul.

Sometimes justice had to be served on the patients if they broke the strict rules of each institution, and penalties were delivered to each offender, such as fines, fasting, or even flogging.

Each resident or patient had a bed, usually a timber frame with rope straps, covered with a mattress of straw, as well as a sheet. Sometimes two people were expected to sleep in one bed. The beds were laid parallel on either side of a long room, known as the infirmary hall.

Men and women were segregated from each other. They often both had a separate infirmary or were divided from each other by a screen.

Residents were expected to work at the hospital, if able to do so, either helping with the laundry, cleaning, tending to the herb and food gardens, orchards, etc, as well as drawing and carrying water from the hospital's well, and helping cook, bake and brew, etc.

Some hospitals had their own farm, so residents were also tasked with the husbandry of the animals, just like the monastic houses had their granges. Some hospitals had dovecotes, and the birds were kept for their eggs as well as meat. Some also had fishponds, much like monasteries and medieval manors had up and down the country.

Each hospital basically had an infirmary hall, a chapel, and accommodation for the master. There would also be a kitchen, a kitchen garden (including herb beds), and sometimes an orchard. Each would also have had its own water well, and was often also near to a local watercourse.

In smaller hospitals, the main building was a long infirmary hall, with the chapel at the east end, and the Master's accommodation at the west, although they may also be separate from each other, and sometimes only consisting of an infirmary and a chapel. Ancillary buildings such as a kitchen, bakehouse, and brewhouse would be located around the main building(s).

Sometimes, especially if a leper hospital, they would also have had a cemetery for those who died at each establishment. They too would also have had walls and gates to make the leper hospital complex secure, so as not to spread leprosy, which was much feared and prevalent in the Middle Ages.

In larger hospitals they would be on par with a monastic house, maybe with a larger infirmary hall, a refectory, a master's house, a dormitory for the brethren and sisters, cloisters, a bell tower, sometimes a dedicated church, or a larger chapel, latrines, as well as other ancillary and service buildings, etc.

The Priory and Medieval Hospitals of Nantwich and Wybunbury, were most likely made up of a complex of timber-framed buildings, possibly with some stone parts or structures, especially St Nicholas' Hospital, where evidence was found that part of it was stone.

Cheshire, like many shires in the Marches, had many medieval churches constructed of timber frames in the past. Locally St Michael's Church at Baddiley, has a timber-framed chancel, whilst its nave has been encased in brick.

St Michael's Church in Coppenhall, now in the town of Crewe, was also originally timber-framed until it was replaced with a brick church. So too was Haslington near Crewe, before it was rebuilt.

Other surviving medieval timber-framed churches in Cheshire, exist at: St Oswald's Church, Lower Peover near Knutsford; St James and St Paul's Church, Marton near Congleton; and All Saints Church, Siddington near Macclesfield.

\* \* \* \* \* \* \*

There were several hundred if not well over a thousand such hospitals in England during the medieval period, usually dating from the Norman Conquest to the time of the Dissolution. Some hospitals did survive the Dissolution, but the majority became dissolved, much like the monasteries, which also provided shelter and care.

Earlier than the Dissolution, the 14th century Black Death affected many hospitals, with many closing down afterward.

St Lawrence's in Nantwich was affected by the Black Death and had no chaplain soon after, possibly he too had died from the devastating plague. Soon after, it is thought that this was why the hospital no longer acted as a house for lepers, as leprosy had begun to decline.

Many also came about due to the Crusades, when the knights who 'took the Cross' brought about a spiritual revival to Europe and beyond.

Wybunbury's Hospital of the Holy Cross and St George, as well as St Lawrence's Hospital in Nantwich, may be examples of medieval hospitals, set up because of the Crusades.

The military religious order of the Knights Hospitaller, were most prevalent in the running and founding of medieval hospitals. The hospital in Jerusalem had cared for many pilgrims as well as Crusaders, and many came back and bequeathed land to the Order, as well as founding hospitals for them. This is likely the case with St Nicholas' Hospital in Nantwich.

* * * * * * *

They were houses of God, and were sometimes called a 'Maison Dieu' or 'Domus Dei', i.e. God's House; because they were really religious communities housed under God.

They were often founded and funded by donations from: royalty; the Church, and its hierarchy; nobles; and merchants; often hoping their good deeds in the eyes of God would be noticed, and their souls and their passage, saved, in the act of Faith, Hope, and Charity.

Those housed in the many hundreds of medieval hospitals up and down the country, generally lived a better life than those who could not be accommodated. Those who were outside of their care must have lived a very hard and painful existence.

When Henry VIII and his advisors brought about the Dissolution, the country never really recovered the charity and care offered by the monasteries, priories, and hospitals, until the reforms of the Victorian period and the advent of the 20$^{th}$ century.

Although we must not forget, the charity of people between those two periods of history, who through their benevolence, set up many almshouses and hospitals by their own or shared means; as well as those who gave alms to the poor and infirm, or left funds at their death, to distribute money or food to the poor and sick.

Today, we must really thank our National Health Service, for we are very lucky in our modern era to be exceptionally cared for, compared to what our ancestors had to suffer and endure, as well as the leaps and bounds over the past two centuries of improved scientific and technological advances.

* * * * * * *

# The Guild of the Holy Cross and Nantwich

The Guild of the Holy Cross was a religious fraternity that also acted as a social organisation for the town's people of Nantwich. Via subscription it raised money to support the townsfolk and in return is believed to have offered support religiously by way of services and prayers, as well as conducting mass for members' dead families and relatives in the chantry chapels of St Mary's. The guild would have also used subscriptions to employ a priest or a number of priests to carry out such services. Funeral ceremonies and their extent could also be under the control of the guild.

They most likely also cared for the poor, as well as for the ill relatives of their members' families, and as such may have been involved to some degree in the running of Nantwich's St Nicholas' and St Lawrence's, Chapels and Hospitals, and Wybunbury's the Holy Cross and St George Hospital, to the south-east of the town.

Guilds also acted to regulate trade and the trade professions in towns, as we see in cities, and the capital London, where many professions have their own specific guild. This would set rules for their members and curbs on those that were not members of the guild. They could set fees each trade could charge and could control apprenticeships to each guild, or those members of a specific town's guild. They also regulated where people could be buried in the local church, and could even officiate over the local guild fair and any ceremonies or plays which would take place at that fair, or other specific religious holidays or saint's day celebrations.

They may have also been involved with Nantwich Priory, if in fact, it was a medieval hospital offering support for those of ill health, much like Nantwich's other two hospitals, albeit for St Lawrence's, later in its history, when it cared for those ill of health, and not just for lepers.

The guild and its brethren also raised money from civil and criminal offences in the town, by fining the perpetrators. They also helped members with the payment of taxes or supported them in matters of law.

According to James Hall in his '**History of Nantwich, 1883, Pages 29, 30 & 32'**, Sir Thomas Fouleshurst, knight, became Sheriff of Chester in 1528, and created a Code of Regulations for the governance of Nantwich ten years later, and included rules regarding the Guild, as shown below in bold:-

*"Clause 6. Alsoe it is ordered that the said ffreehoulders with ye wardens of the Church shall see that all the **gilte prests [guild priests]** shall observe and keepe all such ordinances as be expressed in a certaine booke here afore made and sealed with the Common Seale bearing date the xth of August in the xii [12] yeare of the Raigne of our soueraigne lord King Henrie the eight. [1520]."*

And *" Clause 20. Alsoe it is ordered that all such p'son or p'sons as be in noe **gilde** within this Church that they nor none of their children shall haue at their decease and their bringing home [meaning burial] none of ye ornaments of the Church: nor no more of the bells to be rungen for them but the third Bell: that there be from henceforth noe passing peale here rungen vnder the payne the Clarke to forfeit iiis [3 shillings] iiiid [and 4 pence]. [3/4]."*

Again James Hall mentions guilds and the Guild of Nantwich, in his '**History of Nantwich, 1883, Pages 276-277'**, where he tells us that:-

*"Religious **Gilds** or, Fraternities as they were sometimes called, which were to be found in small country towns as well as in corporate or Cathedral cities. The following interesting deed exhibits a glimpse of social and religious life in the town, when, long before the introduction of Poor Laws, the inhabitants enrolled themselves in societies for purposes of brotherly aid, the distribution of local charity, the sustentation and reparation of the Church, and various other good objects. By this deed two persons were admitted by the Stewards (officials under the President or Dean of **Gild**) into full benefit of the **Gild**, which not only provided for the members in the circumstances of life, but cared for them even after death. The original deed, formerly in the possession of "Mr. Wilbraham of Nantwich," is not now known to be in existence, but a copy in Latin is preserved in*

*Harl. MSS. 2074. f. 166 a. which has a rough drawing of a seal depending therefrom, representing a naked child with outstretched arms, holding what appears to be a flower or branch in each hand. The following is a translation:-*

*"To the beloved holy and devoted children in Christ William Houe any Sibyl his wife, with all others whatsoever.*

*We, William Ruddock and William Lynche stewards [seneschalli] of the **Gilds** or Fraternities of Wich Malbank lawfully deputed send greeting, that by the prayers of the Saints ye may obtain celestial joys: Forasmuch as out of God's gifts to you, you have contributed to the sustentation of the aforesaid **Gilds** and to the six priests in the Church of the Blessed Mary of Wich Malbank aforesaid, for the daily celebration for the brethren sisters and benefactors alive and dead; We freely admit you to the participation of all masses which shall be celebrated in the said church and to all other and singular "cantilenas" [masses chanted] works and prayers which by our brethren are performed: We promise according to the tenor of these presents in life as also in death; and furthermore we concede that after your deaths, prayers for your souls shall be offered by the said priests and brethren of the said **Gilds** with the prayers for those lately deceased; masses, exequies [funeral rites], and prayers being performed as by the brethren is accustomed to be done. In testimony whereof to their children living and dead we append to these presents our seal of office.*

*Dated on the 8th day of January in the year of our Lord 1461."*

*Though the information concerning the number of **Gilds** and their patron Saints is very meagre; it is worthy of note that in 1461 there were no less than six Chantry priests supported by these societies, and probably as many altars in the Church where prayers were daily said. One, called **the Gild of the Holy Cross**, is referred to in an inscription amongst the ancient heraldic glass; and very probably at Nantwich, on the Invention of the Holy Cross [May 3], the annual **Gild Festival** was held, with processions and amusements; just as in the neighbouring villages Wakes were held every year* on the Saints days of their churches, because there were no Religious **Gilds** there to conduct the ceremonies."

James Hall also tells us in his **'History of Nantwich, 1883, Pages 285'**, that there was stained glass relating to the Nantwich Guild in the South Transept of St Mary's, where under the West Wettenhall Window was the following inscription:-

"Orate p. fratribus et sororib; scc. Crucis q'. fererunt ista'. fenestra'."

**Translation:** "Pray for the Brethren and Sisters of the Holy Cross who made this window."

The 'Guild of the Holy Cross' in Nantwich must have been the prevailing guild of the town, for its name to be recorded in historic documents, and also in the name of the medieval hospital at Wybunbury, but other guilds or fraternities are known about, but not by name, from the copy of the manuscript dating to 1461 shows us above.

\* \* \* \* \* \* \*

The Guild of the Holy Cross had its very own Guildhall, which was situated in the north-west corner of St Mary's Graveyard, in the centre of the town, and opposite the Conservative Club Car Park.

After the Dissolution of the Monasteries, the Guildhall became the property of the Crown and was defunct. But was later founded and converted into a Grammar School in 1560, but recorded as such in 1572, by John and Thomas Thrush, woolpackers of London, who were natives of the town. Money was also granted to the new school by other wealthy benefactors of the town.

Although this is disputed by other writers and this school may have been a different edifice in the town, and not specifically the Guildhall. It may also be the case that the Guildhall didn't survive the Great Fire of 1583, but was rebuilt afterward. There is also some confusion to the above, with the grant of ownership of the Guildhall in 1579 below.[116]

We are also told in a Feoffment (a grant of ownership of freehold property) dating to 26 May 1579, after the Dissolution of the Monasteries, that *"Hugh Jones, Citizen and Mercer of London, sells to Richard Wilbraham of Wich Malbanke, Gentleman, and Richard Wrighte of the same, Yeoman, his property in Namptwich near the church there, called the Guildhall, formerly belonging to the Guild or Fraternity, late in the tenure of the churchwardens, to hold of the Queen in free socage, for the consideration [fee] of £10."*[117]

If the Guildhall did in fact survive the Great Fire of Nantwich of 1583, it was inevitably demolished around 1863, when Sir George Gilbert Scott was extensively renovating the church; It was then replaced with a new Grammar School located at Welsh Row Head, which is now residential apartments and known as 'The Old School House' or 108 Welsh Row. This too was replaced by Malbank School further up the road towards the Canal, in 1921.

In 1611 the Old Guildhall, now a Grammar School, if the same building, had an intricately carved and decorated timber-framed two-storey front porch constructed. This was built by Richard Dale who added a panel to record his labours reading:-

*"RICHARD DALE, FREE MASON, WAS THE MASTER CARPENTER IN MAKING THIS BUYLDINGE ANNO DOMINI 1611."*

**The Old Guild Hall and Grammar School
in St Mary's Churchyard, Nantwich**

*Source: A Short History of Nantwich and Neighbourhood,
Miss E. A. Johnson, revised and completed by Roger Russel,
Johnson's Directory, Nantwich, 1902*

The Grammar School's first Master was Randle Kent, who taught at the school from 1572 to 1623. He also left an inscription, but in Latin, reading when translated as:-

*"Randle Kent, high master of this school, out of his great love of sound learning, and his extreme affection for his nature place, at his own expense hath enlarged this Temple of the Muses and gave it this addition".*[118]

\* \* \* \* \* \* \*

We are told in **'The History of Cheshire, Volume 3, George Ormerod, 1882, Page 426'**, that *"the customs and local jurisdiction in use at the Conquest have been noticed in the extract from Domesday. In addition to the court held by the Norman* *barons of Nantwich and their successors, there was formerly a Guild or brotherhood established here for its better regulation. The present school-house in the churchyard was the common-hall of this society, and persons not incorporated in any of its respective confraternities, were not allowed at their decease to have any ornaments of the church, or to have more of the bells rung for them than the third bell. In matters which the guild had no legal power to redress, its members were aided by the court leet; and from its contributions, six perpetual chaplains were provided to say mass, for the brethren and sisters composing it, as appears by a deed bearing date 1461, which is noticed in the account of the church. Among its antient inscriptions, given hereafter from Harl[eian MSS] Manuscripts 2151, will be found one in which this fraternity is described under the appellation of the brethren and sisters of the Holy Cross."*

This shows the power that the Guild or Brethren of the Holy Cross held in the town of Nantwich, as well as their monopoly upon the rituals of burial and the prayers of the mass, of St Mary's Church and its flock.

*Porch of the Grammar School (Old Guildhall),*
*History of Nantwich, James Hall, 1883, Frontispiece*
*(Re-produced from a plate by C. J. Richardson)*

The school-house became vested in the Crown on the suppression of the Guild, which is named before the time of Richard II, and again in 1461, and was brought from Queen

Elizabeth I. It was formerly the Common Hall of the Guild, an ancient timber building, and situated in the church-yard.[119]

This tells us that the Guild of the Holy Cross were present in Nantwich during the reign of Richard II (1377-1399), during the major period of construction of Nantwich St Mary's.

\* \* \* \* \* \* \*

We know from a historic deed dated 9 May 1277, that the Dean and Chapter of Lichfield confirmed that Combermere Abbey held: the churches of Acton [by Nantwich], Sandon [Staffordshire] and Alstonefield [Staffordshire]; the chapels of Wych Malbank [Nantwich], Wrenbury, [Church] Minshull, and Derefold [Dorfold].[120]

We also know from another historic deed, this time dated 20 December 1456, that Combermere Abbey also held the church of Little [Child's] Ercall in Shropshire.[121]

Another deed, this time dated 4 September 1460, that an *"Appointment by Roger Plymmowth, Abbot of the House and Church of our Lady St Mary of Combermere, and the convent of the same, that Randulph of Wylbram as their procurator [their minister in charge of financial affairs], of the Chapel of our Lady St Mary of Nantwiche called the Nantwiche Chirche, for them to collect all the tithes, oblations, obventions, etc., belonging to the said Chapel and to render an account of the same, for 12 years, for which Randulph of Wylbram, is to receive an annual rent of 26 shillings and 8 pence issuing from their lands and tenements in Wyche Malbank [Nantwich], 4 September 1460"* (CALS Ref: DWN/1/21).[122]

This, therefore tells us that St Mary's Church in Nantwich was under the control of the Abbot and monks of Combermere Abbey, so the Guild of the Holy Cross must have subordinately controlled the Church under the Abbey, during this period.

\* \* \* \* \* \* \*

In the *'The Book of the Abbot of Combermere: 1289 to 1529, Edited by James Hall, The Record Society of Lancashire and Cheshire, Volume 31, 1896, Page 56'*, under the rental terrier of Combermere Abbey's properties in Wich Malbanke, dated 1469, we find *"from Robert Sonky, chaplain, for three cottages **near the hall in the graveyard** [prope aulam in cimitorio] lately in the holding of William Sherman the elder, 4 s[hillings]"*. This, therefore tells us that the Guild of the Holy Cross's Guildhall existed in 1469.

\* \* \* \* \* \* \*

We are also told in *'Chester Chantries, etc, The History of Cheshire, Volume 1, George Ormerod, 1882, Page 354'*, that there was a *"Monastery of St. Cross noticed under the collegiate church of St. John, in which it appears to have merged at an early period."* Also on *'Page 313'* we are told that *"another monastic institution was also connected with [the church of St John], on which bishop Tanner makes the following remark in his Notitia Monastica."* *"By the Lincoln Taxation of the temporalities of the clergy made 1291, it should seem as if there had been a collegiate church of the name of THE HOLY CROSS, because under Archidiaconatus Cestriae [Archdiocese of Chester], and immediately before Abbas Cestriae, is this memonrandum: Portionarii ecclesiae prebendalis S. Crucis Cestriae, non habent temporalia, sed omnia quae habent taxantur cum spiritualibus, prout firmiter asserebant: but I have yet met with no other mention of this society, nor of any church in this city, either collegiate or parochial, so dedicated."* ... *"The following extract from the general ecclesiastical survey, [1534-35], will give all the information which there is now any probability of obtaining on the subject. It appears that three stalls in St. John's were called the prebends of the Holy Cross, and that the holders of these were coparceners [persons with an equal share] in certain glebe lands which then continued untied and appropriated to these stalls, as they most probably had been in 1291, from the use of the same term in the valuation of that date. [Footnote: They are first mentioned in the Lichfield Books in 1424; and it will be seen by the Lists that there were four Prebends [portion of the revenue of a collegiate church granted to a canon as his stipend or salary] of the Holy Cross down to, at least, 1501-11.] There can be little doubt on the whole, that some monastic foundation dedicated to the Holy Cross had previously to this merged in the college of St. John's."*

This, therefore tells us that there was a monastic order of the Holy Cross in the City of Chester and that they may have had a monastery in the city. They were definitely operating in Chester and linked with the Church of St John, by the Amphitheatre, from at least the 13th century to the 16th century.

Could this be the same religious order who had a guild at Nantwich?

* * * * * * *

Interestingly, King Edward I, who founded Vale Royal Abbey, is said to have donated a relic of the True Cross to Vale Royal, after Crusading in the Holy Land in 1270.

Also, Sir William Mainwaring of Baddiley and Peover, whose medieval alabaster effigy still exists in the nearby Church of St Mary's at Acton, was believed to have given *"a piece of the holy cross set in wax"* to the church, on his death in 1399,[123] He was a known Crusader, and must have bought the relic back from the Holy Land.

Also, we are told in **'Cheshire and the Crusades, Kathryn Hurlock, Transactions of the Historic Society of Lancashire and Cheshire, Volume 159, 2010, Pages 4 & 5'**, that Geoffrey de Dutton went on Crusade in the thirteenth century, and it is thought he had brought back part of the Holy Cross, which he presented to Norton Priory. He and his family were the principal benefactors of the canons of the Priory. The Priory was also a pilgrimage site.

Kathryn Hurlock also tells us in the same article, on **'Page 5'**, that there was a piece of the True Cross in St John's Church in Chester (by the Amphitheatre), within the Holy Rood, known as the Crucifix of Chester. This *"may have been brought back by Earl Ranulph [of Chester] after his participation in the Fifth Crusade"*. This too was a destination for pilgrims paying homage to the Lord.

Could the Guild or Brethren of the Holy Cross be linked with relics of the Holy Cross housed in Cheshire, if not the whole of England, or even the whole of Europe?

If St Mary's Church at Acton, Vale Royal near Winsford, Norton Priory, near Runcorn, and St John's Church, Chester; had a piece of the Holy Cross, could the Abbey of Combermere and St Mary's Church at Nantwich, also have had a relic? Why else have a Guild dedicated to the Holy Cross controlling mass and prayer at St Mary's, albeit under the direction of Combermere?

***The Holy Cross or Red Fleur-De-Lys Cross,
Representing St Mary the Virgin,
on the Chancel / Sanctuary Floor,
St Mary's Church, Nantwich***

\* \* \* \* \* \* \*

There was also a 'Guild of the Holy Cross' in the Warwickshire medieval market town of Stratford upon Avon, William Shakespeare's birthplace. Their Guild Chapel in the town still exists and dates back to the 13${}^{th}$ century.

The Chapel was built in c1260 and stood next to their Guildhall on the corner of Church Street and Chapel Lane.

It was a medieval social and religious guild that took subscriptions from members for a range of services. Like the Guild of the Holy Cross at Nantwich, it provided mass for the souls of departed members' families and relatives. They also provided income for almshouses, a hospital, a school, and for the poor of the town.

The guild was suppressed like many of the religious orders were during the Dissolution of the Monasteries, as was Nantwich's, but unlike Nantwich, the guild was inherited by Stratford's Corporation by Royal Charter in 1553.

Its Guild Chapel, however, was separate from the town's church, whereas at Nantwich the 'Guild of the Holy Cross' officiated and controlled part of the town's church.

* * * * * * *

This gives a direct parallel to Nantwich and its Guildhall of the Brethren of the Holy Cross, who most likely were also linked with Wybunbury's medieval Hospital of the Holy Cross and St George.

They could possibly have also been linked with Nantwich Priory.

* * * * * * *

Another Guild of the Holy Cross existed in Brimingham and was founded in 1392, and was another social religious organisation, like that at Stratford, and that at Nantwich.

This guild unlike Stratford's, but like Nantwich's, officiated over chantry chapels and priests in the town's church of St Martin's.

Like Nantwich, it was suppressed during the Dissolution, and like Nantwich, its Guildhall became a Grammar School for the town.

* * * * * * *

Also interesting to this study is the 'Maison Dieu' or 'God's House', which was part of the Hospital of the Blessed Mary of Ospringe, at Faversham, near Canterbury, in Kent.

This hospital was founded in 1234 by Henry III, to care for sick, poor, and aged people, on the pilgrimage route to Canterbury.

It was staffed by the 'Brethren of the Holy Cross', who were governed by the rule of St Augustine.

These Brethren of the Holy Cross may be similar to that operating in other parts of the country, and possibly too at Nantwich.

The Hospital of the Holy Cross and St George, at Wybunbury, most likely was part of Nantwich's Brethren or Guild of the Holy Cross. Like the Brethren at Ospringe, they may have had a Master, priests, and sisters, officiating at this hospital, looking after the poor, sick, and old people in the village.

They may have also staffed Nantwich Priory, and possibly even St Lawrence's Hospital after it was converted from a leper hospital to a hospital for the poor and ill of health.

* * * * * * *

It certainly seems likely that these Orders or Guilds or Brethren of the Holy Cross are linked in some way to a religious order, possibly that of the Crossed / Crutched / or Crozier Friars.

They were known also as 'The Canons Regular of the Order of The Holy Cross'.

According to the **'Crutched Friars and Crosiers: The Canons Regular of the Order of the Holy Cross in England and France, J. Michael Hayden, 2013'**, *"before 1600 [the] Crosiers usually referred to themselves as the 'Brethren of the Holy Cross' (Fratres Sancae Crucis in Latin)"* and that *"in England they were known as the Crutched Friars."*

We are also told that *"five of the orders of Brethren of the Holy Cross are well known (to the relatively few historians interested in the topic). In addition to the Crosiers of Belgium, they were the Canons Regular of the Holy Cross of Coimbra (founded in 1131), the Italian Crocigeri (approved by Pope Alexander III in 1169), the Canons Regular of the Holy Cross with a Red Star (or Bohemian Crosiers), founded about 1237 and the Canons Regular of St. Mary of Metrio (often known as the Order of the Holy Cross with the Red Heart), probably founded in Italy in the early thirteenth century, but found mainly in Poland and Lithuania. All of these orders were approved by Rome between the mid-twelfth and early thirteenth centuries. All five adopted the Rule of St. Augustine. All five were canons regular (though the Red Heart Crosiers may have started as mendicants). All but the Portug[u]ese order traced their origins to the Holy Land."*

J. Michael Hayden goes on to tell us: that they were most likely founded sometime between the late 12th and early 13th century, and that they adhered to the Order of St Augustine; and that an anonymous poem about the order's history, appeared in the mid to late 15th century, and suggested that *"the Order of the Holy Cross was founded by the mother of Emperor Constantine, later known as St Helena. After she found the cross of Jesus in Jerusalem, he wrote, she chose twelve men to whom she gave the duty of protecting it. They were to wear a cross on their clothing and were given the name of the Brethren of the Holy Cross."*

Although their origin, is multi-faceted and there is much speculation and conjecture as to their true history.

They are also thought to have lived like the Canons of the Holy Sepulchre, in Jerusalem, during the Crusades, taking care of pilgrims and crusaders. And it may be that like the Knights Hospitaller and the Knights Templar, they were granted and held hospitals and priories in Northern Europe and more specifically in England too.

J. Michael Hayden also tells us that they are thought to have founded a monastery in 1211-12 *"at Clarus Locus [Clairlieu] in the suburbs of Huy [in Liege, Belgium], near a chapel dedicated to St. Theobald, and dedicated that monastery to the Holy Cross."* And that *"in the late thirteenth century the bones of St. Odilia, said to have been discovered in Cologne by a Crosier brother from Paris, were brought to the Huy monastery. The leaders of the monastery used income from pilgrims visiting the shrine containing the relics of St. Odilia to finance the building of an imposing new church dedicated to the Holy Cross."* And that this *"was the fulfilment of the wish of the earliest Crosiers to rebuild the church of the Holy Cross in Jerusalem destroyed in the eleventh century by Seljuk Turks."*

St Odilia became the Crosiers patron saint, replacing St Helena, and was said to have worked miracles for those who had prayed to her, especially those with diseases of the eye.

Their second patron saint does draw a parallel with the locality of Nantwich, because in another history I wrote, titled *'The Devils of Audley, Barthomley and Betley, Charles E. S. Fairey, September 2016 (Revised 2017)'*, and available online @https://sites.google.com/site/charlesfaireyhistorian/publications/the-devils-of-audley-barthomley-and-betley, also concerns a local holy well which was dedicated to St Odilia. She is the patron saint of eye sufferers.

This holy well which is now no more than a spring emerging from a pipe into a water tank used for watering cattle, is still located between Betley and Leycett on a public footpath, near to Adderley Green on Heighley Lane, in North Staffordshire, and near to the M6 motorway.

We are told in the Foreword to *'Betley Parish Registers [1538-1812], Edited by Percy W. L. Adams, 1916, Pages 7-8'*, that *""about the Ottiwells, however, a word must be said. This family name comes, the writer believes, from a place between Betley and Audley, now called the Devil's Well. This was a sacred Well, still believed locally to be "good for the eyes," dedicated to St. Ottilia, whose French name Odille has since the Reformation been corrupted into Old de'il; and so the Devil's Well."*

I went on to say in the above history that *"there is in fact a Saint Odile, and she is also known as St Odille or Ottilia, and was from Alsace, a boundary town in eastern France, next to the Upper Rhine, bordering Germany and Switzerland today. She is believed to have lived between the years of 660 and 720AD, with her feast day being celebrated on the 13th December.*

*As the reference above, she is associated with blindness, and partial sight, and hence the curing of such. This came about via a miraculous event which cured her blindness when a child. According to legend, she was born blind, and therefore shunned by her father, but her mother, took her from Alsace to be brought up by a peasant family, living at Palma. When she was 12 years old, she was taken to a local monastery, where a bishop, assisted by an angel, baptised her Odile, and immediately she recovered her eye sight."*

\* \* \* \* \* \* \*

The Hospital of the Blessed Mary of Ospringe, at Faversham, near Canterbury, in Kent, as we saw above, according to **'The Hospital of St. Mary of Ospringe commonly called Maison Dieu, Charles H. Drake, Archaeologia Cantiana: Transactions of The Kent Archaeological Society, Volume 30, 1914, Pages 34-78'**, tells us on Page 36 that it: *"consisted of a Master and three brethren who were ... secular priests who had taken the vows of the Order of the Holy Cross."* And, according to the Footnote relating to this text, the *"Brethren of the Holy Cross. [was] A religious Order keeping the Au[gu]stin[e] Rule. They may in some way have been connected with either the Hospitallers or the Templars, with one or other of which Orders some authorities have connected this hospital. Their property was, however, held of the king and of him only. The late Mr. J. F. Wadmore in a learned paper on the Hospitallers in Kent (Archaeologia Cantiana, Vol. XXII) makes no reference to this house, nor can I find that the Knights Templars exercised any control over its members or property. A printed pamphlet (in the British Museum) by the Prior of the Templars in London sets forth the advantages of subscribing to the brotherhood and getting the spiritual benefit of association."*

This, therefore tells us that the 'Brethren of the Holy Cross' at Ospringe Hospital in Kent, was in fact the Order known as the Crosiers, as we discussed above. As well as that they were linked with the Knights Hospitallers and the Knights Templar, albeit not in this case, but the latter, encouraged their members to subscribe to the brotherhood [of the Holy Cross] for the spiritual benefit of the association.

Interestingly, the 'Brethren of the Holy Cross' were governed by the rule of St Augustine, and the Dome of the Rock, on Temple Mount in Jerusalem, was under the jurisdiction of the Augustinian Canons Regular. They converted the mosque into a Christian church, after the capture of the city in 1099. Their neighbours on the Mount were the Knights Templar, who also believed the octagonal Dome was the site of the Holy of Holies of the Temple of Solomon, and where their name derived from.

* * * * * * *

The coat of arms of Nantwich Priory certainly is in a similar vein; and the Hospital at Wybunbury, certainly links to the Crusaders, with half of its dedication being to the Crusader's Saint George, as well as St George's Chapel in the South Transept of St Mary's Church in Nantwich; with both establishments also being dedicated or with a chantry chapel to the latter, to the Holy Cross.

* * * * * * *

There was also a group of Friars who titled themselves 'Brethren of the Holy Cross', present in Paris, during the reign of the saintly King Louis IX (1214-1270). They were said to wear a cross on their chests, and Louis gave them property in Temple Crossing in the French capital city, and the street is still known as 'the Holy Cross'.

* * * * * * *

According to **'Guilds and Related Organisations in Great Britain and Ireland: A Bibliography, Part 1: Introduction, The London Guilds; and Part 2: The English Provincial Guilds, The Irish Guilds, The Scottish Guilds, The Welsh Guilds; compiled by Tom Hoffman, 2011'**, we find that the following establishments refer to a guild called the Holy Cross in London:-

- The Gild of the Holy Cross founded in 1370 (at St. Lawrence Jewry [in Cheap Ward]);
- St Vedast, in Farrington Ward Within, where a gild was established in 1393, and dedicated to the Holy Cross;

And in the rest of Great Britain:-

- Abingdon (Berkshire) In 1442 Richard II granted a charter to the Guild of the Holy Cross, but this guild died out with the other religious guilds in 1547. This guild met at St. Helen's Church, Abingdon. The brethren of this guild obtained a licence from Henry V to build two bridges across the Thames;

- Amcotts (Lincolnshire) The Gild of the Holy Cross founded in 1377-8;
- Birmingham (West Midlands) The religious Guild of the Holy Cross was granted a licence by Richard II in 1392;
- Bishop's Lynn (Norfolk) There were nine religious guilds, one of which was the Gild of the Holy Cross;
- Chesterfield (Derbyshire) The Guild of the Holy Cross of the Merchants of Chesterfield, later to become the Company of Merchants;
- Colchester (Essex) Note on the Licence (1408) to found the Guild of St. Helen in the Chapel of the Holy Cross;
- Eckington (Derbyshire) The Gild of St. Mary and the Holy Cross founded in 1310;
- Ely (Cambridgeshire) The Gild of the Holy Cross founded circa 1374 (in the Church of St. Peter);
- Grantham (Lincolnshire) The Gild of the Exaltation of the Holy Cross founded in 1379 (in the Parish Church); The Gild of the Invention of the Holy Cross founded in 1347 (in the Parish Church);
- Hultoft (Lincolnshire) The Gild of the Holy Cross founded in 1350;
- Icklingham (Suffolk) The Gild of the Holy Cross founded in 1366;
- Lincoln (Lincolnshire) The Gild of the Holy Cross (the Archers) was founded in 1379, where only Archers could hold office in the Gild; The Gild of the Holy Cross (the Fullers) with Statutes dated 1297;
- Luddington (Lincolnshire) The Gild of the Holy Cross founded in 1377-8;
- Lynn (Norfolk) The Gild of the Exaltation of the Holy Cross (the Shipman's Gild) founded in 1368; The Gild of the Holy Cross; The Gild of St. Mary and the Holy Cross;
- Rotherham (Yorkshire) The Gild of the Holy Cross founded in 1356;
- Sawston (Cambridgeshire) The Gild of the Invention of the Holy Cross;
- Shrewsbury (Shropshire) Abbey of the Holy Cross;
- Stratford upon Avon (Warwickshire) The Guild of the Holy Cross;
- Swaffham (Norfolk) The Gild of the Invention of the Holy Cross;
- Swaffham Bulbeck (Cambridgeshire) The Gild of the Holy Cross;
- Tydd St. Giles (Cambridgeshire) The Gild of the Holy Cross founded in 1385-6;

- Upwell (Norfolk) The Gild of the Invention of the Holy Cross (at the Church of St. Peter);
- Walsoken (Norfolk) The Gild of the Holy Cross founded in 1387 (at the Church of All Saints);
- Wermigay (Norfolk) The Gild of the Invention of the Holy Cross;
- and Wormegay (Norfolk) The Gild of the Invention of the Holy Cross (at the Church of St. Michael);

(**Source:** **'Guilds and Related Organisations in Great Britain and Ireland: A Bibliography, compiled by Tom Hoffman, 2011'**).

\* \* \* \* \* \* \*

It is very unlikely due to the scarcity of relevant medieval historic records that we will ever be able to confirm whether the Guild or Brethren of the Holy Cross at Nantwich, is in fact a Crosier Order, or similar.

Therefore it must remain that it is:-

- most likely a religious town guild, which was most likely also linked with the Hospital of the Holy Cross and St George at nearby Wybunbury;

- but there is a possibility that the Holy Cross was a distinct religious Order, which also formed a Guild at Nantwich, related and linked to the Crosiers or Crutched Friars;

- there is also a slight possibility that they were linked with the lost establishment at the head of Welsh Row in the town, known as 'Namptwich Priory', and whose coat of arms is rather similar to the staffs this or these related Orders are often linked with, and symbolised as using.

\* \* \* \* \* \* \*

# Endnotes & References

**1.** Thomas son of Hugh of Wich Malbank grants land between, the land of Radulph de Vernon, the land of Nicholas Cawel? In Hospital Street of Wich Malbank, to William of Edlaston, circa 1300 (Cheshire Archives and Local Studies or CALS Ref: DCH/Z/4).

**2.** A History of the County of Chester: Volume 3: Religious Houses, 1980, Pages 124-127.

**3.** Robert de Marchumleye petitioned the King that he has been assaulted whilst travelling and wounded to the point of death by the wrongdoers, Crump, Rodene and Smute. He seeks redress from the king, c1307-1310 (National Archives Kew, Ref: SC 8/48/2355).

**4.** Lease, for twenty years to begin at Pentescost, [1321], of saltworks in Nantwich, 1321 (Staffordshire Record Office or SRA Ref: D593/A/1/28/9); and Lease, for twenty years to begin at Pentecost, [1321], of saltworks in Nantwich, c1321 (SRA Ref: D593/A/1/28/10).

**5.** Dispute between: Prior and Convent of St. Thomas by Stafford of Order of St. Augustine, appellants; and Robert de Marchumley, clerk, keeper or master of Hospital of St. Nicholas of Wych Malbane, William de Prayers, priest, and Richard de Dodington, Richard de Prayers and Ralph de Taylor, layment, defendants. Concerning tithes of ALDELYME. Prior and convent had held parish church and both greater and lesser tithes until despoiled by Robert de Marchumley and the others of tithes of sheaves in a place commonly called Oxebruggehay, 17 December 1326 (Staffordshire Record Office (SRA) Ref: D938/628b); and Dispute between: Prior and Convent of St. Thomas the Martyr of Order of St. Augustine, by their Proctor, Brother Henry de Wasteneys, canon; and Robert de Marchumleye, Master of Hospital of Wych Malbanc, by his Proctor Nicholas Pollard, clerk; and William de Prayers, priest, Richard de Dodingcton , Richard de Prayers and Ralph le Taylour, laymen of diocese of Coventry and Lichfield by their Proctor John de Poulton. Concerning tithes of place called Oxebruggehay in parish of ALDELYME [Audlem, co. Chester] claimed by Prior and Convent, following receipt (recited) of Pope John XXII dated 29 June 1325. Referring also to the churches of STOWE BY CHARTLEY, CAVERSWALL and MAER which the Prior and Convent also hold to their own uses, 17 December 1326 (SRA Ref: D938/19).

**6.** Cheshire Sheaf, 3rd Series, Vol 20, June 27, 1923, Notes, Article 4812 The Domesday Roll of Chester, Page 53.

**7.** Cheshire Sheaf, 3rd Series, Vol 55, August 6, 1960, Notes, Article 10,653, Bishop Stretton's Register, Archdeaconry of Chester, 1364, Page 72.

**8.** Cheshire Sheaf, 3rd Series, Vol 55, August 27, 1960, Notes, Article 10,665, Bishop Stretton's Register, Archdeaconry of Chester, 1374, Page 79.

**9.** Grant of Robert of Fouleshurst of Edlaston to David le Wright of Ridley, two places of land with their buildings in Wich Malbank, of which ... the other part of land lies in length between the high street and the orchard of the Hospital of St. Nicholas, and in width between the land which was that of Thomas Sharp on the one part and the land which William le Webb held of the aforesaid Robert at the time of this making on the other side, 11 June 1374 (CALS Ref: DCH/Z/10).

**10.** A History of the County of Chester: Volume 3, Victoria County History, 1980, Pages 186-187. & Wills & Inventories, i (Surtees Soc. 1835 (2)), 52, Emden, Biog. Reg. Oxford, ii. 13545.

**11.** Matilda, Widow of John Cheswys, appoints Henry Bradfield, her Attorney, present to Richard Golborn of Henhull all that part of land of a wich-house of 12 leads in the Wich, between a street called le Wodestrete on the east, and the common cistern on the west, and between the land of Thomas son of John Wettenhall on the south, and land of the Hospital of St. Nicholas the Bishop on the north. 12 May 1468 (CALS Ref: DCH/Z/7).

**12.** Grant of Adam Wettenhall of Acton to John Wettenhall of Wich Malbank, all that place of land of mine with its buildings lying in Wich Malbank between the King's high street leading towards Acton on the south side and the land of the Hospital of St. Nicholas on the north side, and between a certain lane called le Porteslone [Porch Lane, now known as Red Lion Lane, and next to the site of the ancient house known as the Porch House] on the east side and the land of Robert Fouleshurst, knight, on the west side, 24 August 1486 (Chetwode Papers, Keele University Ref: CH 219).

**13 & 16.** The History of Cheshire, Volume 3, George Ormerod, 1882, Page 424; and Harleian Manuscripts 1967, Entry 118.

**14.** Sir Robert Fouleshurst of Crewe grants a messuage in Nantwich to John Brooke of Leighton, of one messuage lying in Wich Malbank in the high street leading towards the bridge on the east side of the said street, lately called le Bell, in length between the said street and land lately that of Richard Wildebore, and in width between land lately that of Hugh Wettenhall on the north side and land lately that of Thomas Stooke on the south side at the west end of the said messuage, and between land of the said Thomas Stooke on the north side and land of the Hospital of St. Nicholas and land of the heirs of William Glaseley on the south side, 1 May 1489 (Chetwode Papers, Keele University Ref: CH 327).

**15.** Grant of Richard Golborn of Henhull to Sir William Stanley and William Wilbraham of Woodhey, of one half of a wich-house of 12 leads lying in Wich Malbank between a certain street called le Wodestrete on the east, and the common cistern on the west, and between the land of Thomas son of John Wettenhall on the south, and the land of [the Hospital of] St. Nicholas the Bishop on the north, 25 November 1494 (CALS Ref: DCH/Z/15).

**16.** See 13 above.

**17.** Bargain and Sale by Richard Wrighte of the Wiche Malbanke al. Namptwiche to Roger Wilbram son of Rychard Wilbram of the sd. Wich --- all the tithes of flax, hemp, pigs and all other garden tithes arising in all houses, gardens and other tenements in the WICHE aforesaid, viz. in the late hospitall of Sente Nicholas and all lands and tenements belonging to the same; all houses, gardens etc. on the south side of the Welshe Rowe, the South and west sides of the highe towne and the North side of the Milne strete, out of which the said late hospitall of St. Nicholas lately had/now hath/of right ought to have, 2 parts of the tithes of flax, hemp and pigs; to hold of the Queen as of her Manor of Est Grenewiche (Co. Kent) in free socage, 18 October 1569 (CALS Ref: DWN/2/95).

**18.** Agreement between: William Pearetree, clerk, executor of John Thrush, late of Wich Malbanke, gentleman, deceased, and John Farrar of Wich Malbanke, shoemaker, one of the younger sons of John Farrar, gentleman, deceased, late son in law to the sd. John Thrush; and Roger Wilbraham of Wich Malbanke Esq.; reciting that WHEREAS the sd. William Pearetree has by Indenture of 4. Apr. 1654 assigned to the sd. John Farrar the son, one croft with appurtenances called St. Anns croft, late in the holding of the sd. John Thrush, for the residue of a term determinable on the decease of Roger Wilbraham of Darfould Esq., and WHEREAS there is now in arrear to Roger Wilbraham, party to these presents, the sum of £55-12-8 for rent out of the sd. croft and other premises heretofore belonging to the Hospital of St. Nicholas in WICH MALBANKE, the reversion whereof now belongs to the sd. Roger Wilbraham and his heirs, NOW the sd. William Pearetree and John Farrar, in consideration of the sd. £55-12-8 are agreed that the sd. Roger Wilbraham shall henceforward hold the sd. croft until such time as he shall out of the annual profits have received the sd. sum of £55-12-8, 7 April 1654 (CALS Ref: DWN/2/155).

**19.** Lease for 69 years, by Richard Wilberham of the Wiche Malbanke to Thomas Clutton of the sd. Wiche --- the tithe corn, hay, hemp, flax, wood and kidds of the township and fields of LEIGHTON, late in the tenure of Roger Broke, and also all that his part of 1 pasture in the parish of ACTON called Seint Anne croft or hospitall croft and all his part of the tithe corn of the township and fields of NEWBOLD, at an annual rent of 40/-. Cons. £22-6-8, 1 June 1555 (CALS Ref: DWN/2/85).

**20 & 22.** Lease for 3 lives by Roger Wilbraham of Wiche Malbancke Esq. to William Jackson of the same, tanner, a messuage/tenement and garden thereto adjoining with appurts. called St. Nicholas Hospitall in WICH MALBANCKE, now in the holding of the sd. William Jackson; for lives of the sd. William Jackson, Richard Jackson his son and William Steele, son of Thomas Steele of Cholmondeley, yeoman, at annual rent of £2-13-4; the lessee covenants at his own cost to erect a sufficient tanhouse on some part of the premises, to sink the necessary pits and to make 2 sufficient gates for the way leading to the sd. hospithall croft for the sd. Roger, 25 December 1655 (CALS Ref: DWN/2/157).

**21.** Nantwich Pubs, Andrew Lamberton and Bill Pearson, 2018, Page 121.

**22.** See 20 above.

**23.** A History of the Town and Parish of Nantwich or Wych-Malbank, Cheshire, James Hall, 1883 (Republished 1972), Page 53.

**24.** Grant of William of Poole to Richard son of Robert Coterel of Poole (later 13th century?) of [a pound of?] cumin which I had of the Hospital in the vill of Wich Malbank each year in [...] street. (CALS Ref: DMW 6/27).

**25.** Rental of lands belonging to the Knights and Hospitallers of St. John of Jerusalem and of the lands of Robert Salamon, Nantwich area, c.1380-1390 (CRO Ref: DDX350).

**26, 28, 31 & 37.** Copie of an old Rental of the Commandery of Ivelie in the Countie of Chester formerly belonging to the Knights Hospitallers of St. John of Jerusalem in England. Harleian Manuscript, MS 1999, Entry 6, 18.a, (Folios 21r-30v). (Catalogue of the Harleian Manuscripts in the British Museum, Volume II, 1808, MS 1999, Entry 6, 18.a, Page 379).

**27.** Deed to premises in Monson, Wardley, Pendleton, Lancashire; Lavenham and Long Melford, Suffolk; Walton on the Naze, Essex; Richmond, Surrey, including deed relating to rights of Hospital of St John of Jerusalem in Middlewich Fee, 1576/1609 (CRO Ref: DCH/P/4).

**28.** See 26 above.

**29 & 32.** Deeds Relating to Early Tenures of Land, &c., in Minshull Vernon and Adjacent Townships in Cheshire, Frank Renaud, Pages 49-62, Transactions of the Lancashire and Cheshire Antiquarian Society, Volume 15, 1898.

**30.** Gifts to Mobberley Priory, Four Salt Pits in Northwich, held of the Hospital of St. John of Jerusalem, c.1206 (CRO Refs: DDX553/1-4).

**31.** See 26 above.

**32.** See 29 above.

**33.** 1550. Page 259, Hospitallers of St. John of Jerusalem, The Cheshire Sheaf, 1st Series, Volume 2, 1883.

**34 & 40.** The Cheshire Sheaf, various: 1482. Page 231, 1497. Page 238, 1550. Page 259, 1st Series, Volume 2, 1883; 2029. Page 57, 1st Series, Volume 3, 1891; 1484. Page 97, 3rd Series, Volume 7, 1910; 2266. Page 61, 3rd Series, Volume 10, 1914; 2950. Page 78, 3rd Series, Volume 12, 1917; 3465. Page 77, 3rd Series, Volume 14, 1919; 4069. Page 56, 3rd Series, Volume 17, 1922; 4712. Page 10, 3rd Series, Volume 20, 1924; 5718. Page 66-67, 5742. Page 81, 3rd Series, Volume 25, 1931; 6662. Page 62, 3rd Series, Volume 30, 1936; 8681. Page 12, 3rd Series, Volume 41, 1947.

**35.** The Charters of the Anglo-Norman Earls of Chester, C.1071-1237, Geoffrey Barraclough, The Record Society of Lancashire and Cheshire, Volume 126, 1988, Page 192-193.

**36.** The Lesser-known Gatehouses and Gateways of Lancashire and Cheshire, James A. Waite, The Historic Society of Lancashire & Cheshire, Volume 50, 1898, Pages 77-110.

**37.** See 26 above.

**38.** Nantwich: Saxon to Puritan, Eric Garton, 1972, Page 77, and Footnote 5. Grant P.R.O. E318 8/11.

**39.** Views of Accounts of King's Ministers etc. of late monasteries in Cheshire; Birkenhead, Norton, Combermere, Vale Royal, Preceptory of Yeveley, (Derbyshire), Bassingwerk, parcel of possessions of late William Stanley, knight, Lenton, late monastery in Norfolk, parcel of possessions of bishopric of Chester in King's hands by exchange, 25 July 1555 to 5 July 1558 (National Archives, Kew, Ref: E 315/453/2).

**40.** See 34 above.

**41.** No. 8 – An Unusual Architectural Feature in St Mary's Church, Nantwich, Cheshire Past: An Annual Review of Archaeology in Cheshire, Issue 4, Cheshire County Council, 1995.

**42.** The Knights Templar Chapel, Onneley, North Staffordshire, Charles E. S. Fairey, December 2013 (Revised 2015).
See https://sites.google.com/site/charlesfaireyhistorian/publications/knights-templar-chapel-onneley.

**43.** Notes on the Churches of Cheshire, Sir Stephen R. Glynne, Baronet, Chetham Society, Volume 32, 1894, Pages 1-7.

**44.** Cheshire Sheaf, 3rd Series, Vol 20, June 27, 1923, Notes, Article 4812 The Domesday Roll of Chester, Page 53.

**45.** Rental of lands belonging to the Knights and Hospitallers of St. John of Jerusalem and of the lands of Robert Salamon, Nantwich area, c.1380-1390 (CRO Ref: DDX350.

**46, 47 & 49.** Grant by William Colfox to Nicholas, his son, of tenements in Wyco Malbano [Nantwich], in le Beinstrete in exchange for land, with buildings, in le Hospitelstrete, 8 April 1339 (National Archives, Kew, Ref: C 146/6687); Grant of land and salt-works in Nantwich, by John son of Thomas Joel, to Richard de Fouleshurst, 19 September 1353 (National Archives, Kew, Ref: C 146/6692); Grant by Walter de Upston and others to Ralph de Brunham, 14 Richard II [1390/91] (National Archives, Kew, Ref: E 329/338); Demise by John Touchet, Lord of Tatenhale to William Partryche of one piece of ground in Wich Malban [Nantwich], 5 May 1393 (CALS Ref: DWN/2/24); Petition of Nicholas Colfox, Knight, to the King, relating to Thomas of Woodstock, Duke of Gloucester, 1404 (National Archives, Kew, Ref: SC 8/254/12671); Grant by Pelerina, formerly wife of Robert le Massy de Hale, to Thomas Maysturson the elder, of 2 pieces of land in Wych Malban [Nantwich], 7 September 1425 (CALS Ref: DWN/1/14).

**47.** See 46 above.

**48.** A History of the County of Chester: Volume 5 Part 1, the City of Chester: General History and Topography: Later medieval Chester 1230-1550: City and crown, 1350-1550, Pages 55-58.

**49.** See 46 above.

**50.** The Earldom and County Palatine of Chester, Geoffrey Barraclough, The Journal of the Historic Society of Lancashire and Cheshire, Volume 103, 1951, Pages 23-57. Page 43.

**51.** Reign of Richard II, *272; Calendar Close Rolls, 1396-9, 382.*

**52.** A Short History of Nantwich and Neighbourhood, Miss E. A. Johnson, revised and completed by Roger Russel, Johnson's Directory, Nantwich, 1902.

**53 & 54.** The Military Personnel of Edward the Black Prince, David S. Green, Medieval Prosopography, Volume 21, 2000, Page 137; and Public Record Office, E101/29/24; P.J. Morgan, "Cheshire and the Defence of the Principality of Aquitaine," Transactions of the Historical Society of Lancashire and Cheshire, Volume 128 (1978), Pages 148-49. In the roll the Cheshire contingent is grouped into three sections: a block of five esquires leading seventy archers; seven knights with men-at-arms plus forty archers (four of whom served at Poitiers); and individual men-at-arms.

**54.** See 53 above.

**55.** Acton (Near Nantwich): The History of a Cheshire Parish and its seventeen townships, Edited by Frank A. Latham, 1995, Page 65.

**56, 63 & 67.** A Guide to The Church of S. Mary's, Nantwich, Cheshire, by Percy Newton Corry, May 1962.

**57 & 64.** Tracing the Past: Medieval Vaults: Nantwich https://www.tracingthepast.org.uk/2021/04/08/nantwich_site_by_site/, and https://www.tracingthepast.org.uk/2021/04/08/nantwich_history/.

**58.** Master Masons of the Diocese of Lichfield: A Study in 14th Century Architecture at the Time of the Black Death, JM Maddison, Transactions of the Lancashire and Cheshire Antiquarian Society, Volume 85, 1988 (with Notes).

**59.** Calendar of Patent Rolls 1381–5, 228; 2nd Reg. Stretton, 148.

**60.** A History of the County of Chester: Volume 3. Originally published by Victoria County History, London, 1980, Pages 150-156.

**61.** History of Combermere Abbey: http://www.combermere-restoration.co.uk/the-wicked-monks-of-combermere/.

**62.** Confirmation by the Dean and Chapter of Lichifield, on behalf of Roger Bishop of Coventry and Lichfield, of which churches and chapels Combermere Abbey holds in Cheshire and Staffordshire, 9 May 1277 (CALS Ref: D5589/1).

**63.** See 56 above.

**64.** See 57 above.

**65.** A History of the County of Chester: Volume 5 Part 1, the City of Chester: General History and Topography: Later medieval Chester 1230-1550: City and crown, 1350-1550, Pages 55-58.

**66.** The Military Personnel of Edward the Black Prince, David S. Green, Medieval Prosopography, Volume 21, 2000, Page 135; & Public Record Office, SC6/772/5, Cheshire chamberlain accounts, 1369-70. Total annuities, £1,537 7s. 6d. By 1374 this had fallen to £1,245 2d. out of a total income of £2,523 17s. 2d. (SC6/772/10).

**67.** See 56 above.

**68.** W. Wonnacott, "Henry Yevely," Ars Quattuor Coronatorum, XXI, 1908.

**69.** Keele's Templar Window: and the Templars Jacques de Molay & Thomas Totty, Robin Studd, 2018, Page 98-101.

**70.** A History of the County of Chester: Volume 5 Part 1, the City of Chester: General History and Topography: Later medieval Chester 1230-1550: City and crown, 1350-1550, Pages 55-58.

**71.** A History of the Town and Parish of Nantwich or Wych-Malbank, Cheshire, James Hall, 1883 (Republished 1972).

**72.** Nantwich: Saxon to Puritan, Eric Garton, 1972, Page 10.

**73.** Nantwich: Saxon to Puritan, Eric Garton, 1972, Page 13.

**74 & 75.** Nantwich: Saxon to Puritan, Eric Garton, 1972, Page 14.

**75.** See 74 above.

**76 & 77.** Nantwich: Saxon to Puritan, Eric Garton, 1972, Page 15.

**77.** See 76 above.

**78.** Nantwich: Saxon to Puritan, Eric Garton, 1972, Pages 17 & 20.

**79.** A History of the Town and Parish of Nantwich or Wych-Malbank, Cheshire, James Hall, 1883 (Republished 1972).

**80.** Gift by Sir David Cradok, k[nigh]t., to Sir Nicholas de Haselynton, chaplain, of all his lands, tenements and rents in Nantwich, 8 Jul. 1366 (CALS Ref: DDX553/41).

**81.** GRANT by Ralph s. of William de Wylbram Nicholas de Haselyntton chaplain and Richard s. of Roger del Hope to Thomas le Maistersone sen. in tail male of all those messuages lands tenements rents etc which they formerly held in vill and territory of WICH MALBANK by feoffment of Robert Maistersone and also all lands with appurtenances in vill of HENHULL also formerly held by them of his feoffment with remainder in default of male heir to Richard s. of David Cradok knight & failing his heir to those of Roger brother of sd. Richard s. of David and failing his heir to male heirs of sd. Ralp s. of William de Wilbram and failing an heir to him to the right heirs of sd. Robert de Maistersone. Witnesses: Laurence de Dutton knight then Sheriff of Cheshire, Robert de Foulesrhurst, William de Praers, Richard de Henhull, William s. of Richard de Marthunleg, 16 March 1371/2 (CALS Ref: DBW/A/I/1).

**82.** Nantwich: Saxon to Puritan, Eric Garton, 1972, Page 20.

**83.** Nantwich: Saxon to Puritan, Eric Garton, 1972, Pages 20 & 21.

**84.** Nantwich: Saxon to Puritan, Eric Garton, 1972, Pages 16, 20 & 23.

**85.** Saint Mary's Parish Church, Nantwich, R. E. Pritchard, No Date (after 1973), Page 10.

**86 & 87.** The History of Cheshire, Volume 3, George Ormerod, 1882, Page 424; and Harleian Manuscripts, 1967, Entry 118.

**87.** See 86 above.

**88.** Inventories of Church Goods and Chantries in Cheshire, Temp Edward VI., The Historic Society of Lancashire and Cheshire, Volume 23 (1870-1872), Rev. Mackenzie E. C. Walcott, 27 January 1870, Pages 179.

**89, 91 & 101.** William Kirkham and Thomas Kirkham, of Gray's Inn, Middlesex (Grantor) to Thomas Tettnall, of Tattenhall, Gentleman (Grantee), 30 Eliz I (1588) (National Archives, Kew; Ref C147/315).

**90, 91 & 101.** Indenture of Sale by William Kirkham and Thomas Kirkham of Gray's Inn, Middlesex, Gentlemen, to John Mere of Mere, co. Chester, Esquire, and Henry More of Weley, co. Chester, 32 Eliz I (1590) (National Archives, Kew; Ref WALE 30/40).

**91.** See 89 and 90 above.

**92.** An Estate Account Book of Thomas Wilbraham, with accounts and receipts, 1655-81, rents for hospital houses, 1842-58, and receipts from wallings, 1658-61 (DBW/P/J/6).

**93 & 94 & 102.** Tollemache (Wilbraham of Woodhey) Collection: Summary of an Estate in Acton and Hurleston, also Wilbraham's hospital in Nantwich, 1599-1954, (CALS Ref: DTW/A).

**94.** See 93 above.

**95 & 112.** Feoffment by Sir Francis Newporte of Highe Ercoll (Co. Salon), Kt., to Sir Roger Wilbraham Kt., one of the Masters of Requests in Ordinary to the King and Surveyor of H.M.'s Court of Wards and Liveries --- a parcel of land called the hospitall yard in WICHE MALBANCKE now in the tenure of Raphe Wilbraham, gentleman, on the East adjoining lands of the inheritance of the sd. Sir Francis Newporte, on the West lands of the heirs of Richard Wright, late of the Bell in Wich Malbancke, deceased, on the South the high way or pavement from the said Wiche towards Acton Church, and on the North lands of the inheritance of the sd. Sir Francis. Cons. £10, 29 April 1612 (CALS Ref: DWN/2/124).

**96.** Assignment of Lease by Richard Wilbraham of Wiche Malbanke, gentleman, to Rauffe Wilbraham, his son --- a messuage/tenement/hospital in the WICHE called the hospitall, 1 cottage there wherein Roberte Boyer now dwells, another cottage there now in the tenure of Marryan Cretchley, 1 pasture/crofte there called the hospitall crofte and another croft there called Saincte Anne Crofte alias Froggreaves (except 9 butts in the West end thereof being the narrow end which are of the inheritance of Rauffe Wilbraham, gentleman, son of the sd. Richard), 1 wichhouse of 12 leads there in a place called greate wood streete and the site/ground of 1 wich house of 6 leads in Pepper streete in WICHE aforesaid, all which premises are now in the tenure of the sd. Richard Wilbraham; for lives of the sd. Rauffe Wilbraham, Roger Wilbraham his son, and Thomas Wilbraham, son of Richard Wilbraham, son and heir of the sd. Richard Wilbraham, at an annual rent of £8, 40 strike of well made white salt of Shrewsburie measure heaped, or 20d. per strike in lieu thereof, and 6 Namptwiche cheeses to be made within Wiche Malbanke aforesaid, every cheese to contain 16lbs. weight. to hold for the residue of the term therein mentioned, 12 May 1598 (CALS Ref: DWN/2/116).

**97 & 103.** Lease by Francis Newporte of High Arcoll (Co. Salop), Esq., to Richard Wilbraham of Wiche Malbanke, gentleman --- a messuage/tenement/hospital in the WICHE called the hospitall, 1 cottage there wherein Roberte Boyer now dwells, another cottage there now in the tenure of Marryan Cretchley, 1 pasture/crofte there called the hospitall crofte and another croft there called Saincte Anne Crofte alias Froggreaves (except 9 butts in the West end thereof being the narrow end which are of the inheritance of Rauffe Wilbraham, gentleman, son of the sd. Richard), 1 wichhouse of 12 leads there in a place called greate wood streete and the site/ground of 1 wich house of 6 leads in Pepper streete in WICHE aforesaid, all which premises are now in the tenure of the sd. Richard Wilbraham; for lives of the sd. Rauffe Wilbraham, Roger Wilbraham his son, and Thomas Wilbraham, son of Richard Wilbraham, son and heir of the sd. Richard Wilbraham, at an annual rent of £8, 40 strike of well made white salt of Shrewsburie measure heaped, or 20d. per strike in lieu thereof, and 6 Namptwiche cheeses to be made within Wiche Malbanke aforesaid, every cheese to contain 16lbs. Weight, 19 May 1597 (CALS Ref: DWN/2/114).

**98.** Agreement between Richard Wilbraham of Wichemalbanke, gent., and Rauffe Wilbraham his son and Margarett Maynwaringe of Wiche Malbanke, widow; whereby, after reciting the Settlement made on the marriage of the sd. Rauffe Wilbraham and Ales now his wife, daughter of the sd. Margarett Maynwaringe (18. Aug. 1581), a lease for 3 lives made by Frauncis Newporte of Highe Arcall (Co. Salop), Esq. to the sd. Richard Wilbraham (19. May 1597) and the Assignment of the sd. lease in reversion by the sd. Richard Wilbraham to the sd. Rauffe Wilbraham (12. May 1598), wherein the sd. Richard covenanted that he would by his last will and testament or otherwise bequeath to the sd. Rauffe ¼ of all his moveable goods and of the debts owing to him (except as excepted); and reciting that since that time the sd. Rauffe has had some doubt as to whether the sd. Richd. might give many great legacies in his will, thereby leaving only a small remnant of his moveable goods and debts, now it is agreed that the sd. Richard shall give to the sd. Rauffe the sum of £100, in consideration of which the sd. Rauffe Wilbraham and Margarett Maynwaringe have released the sd. Richard from all and singular the foresd. covenants, promises and agreements and all actions, suits and demands against him, 14 January 1608/9 (CALS Ref: DWN/1/73).

**99.** Agreement between 1) William Pearetree, clerk, executor of John Thrush, late of Wich Malbanke, gentleman, deceased, and John Farrar of Wich Malbanke, shoemaker, one of the younger sons of John Farrar, late of Wich Malbanke, gentleman deceased, and 2) Roger Wilbraham of Wich Malbanke, Esq.; reciting that WHEREAS the sd. John Thrush being lawfully possessed of a messuage called the Hospital now divided into 3 dwellings in/near the Welsh Row in WICH MALBANKE and 1 pasture/croft called the Hospitall croft in WICH MALBANKE and 1 wich house of 12 leads and the walling thereto belonging in Great wood street in WICH MALBANKE and in annual rents of 10/s issuing out of 2 cottages now in the holding of William Pratchett the elder, butcher, in the Pepper Street in WICH MALBANKE, 6/8 out of a cottage/burgage in the High Towne there wherein Raphe Deane now dwelleth, 2/- out of 2 other cottages and an orchard in the Welsh Rowe now in the holding of Roger Bickerton, for a term of years, did make his will and thereby devised the sd. premises to the sd. William Pearetree to the purposes therein declared, the reversion of which premises with the annual rents and services belonged to Thomas Wilbraham deceased, late father to the sd. Roger Wilbraham, NOW it is agreed that the sd. Roger Wilbraham and his heirs may from henceforth annually during the residue of the sd. term occupy and enjoy the sd. messuage, pasture and rents, and the sd. John Farrar covenants to pay 40/- annually (to be issuing out of the sd. wich house and walling) to the sd. Roger Wilbraham, his heirs and assigns, in lieu of the rents and services due for the entire premises, for the residue of the term, 20 August 1653 (CALS Ref: DWN/2/154).

**100.** Assignment by Raphe Wilbraham of Derfolde, Esq. to John Thrushe of Wich Malbanke, gentleman, and Thomas Bickerton of the same, yeoman --- a messuage/tenement/hospital in the WICHE called the hospitall, 1 cottage there wherein Roberte Boyer now dwells, another cottage there now in the tenure of Marryan Cretchley, 1 pasture/crofte there called the hospitall crofte and another croft there called Saincte Anne Crofte alias Froggreaves (except 9 butts in the West end thereof being the narrow end which are of the inheritance of Rauffe Wilbraham, gentleman, son of the sd. Richard), 1 wichhouse of 12 leads there in a place called greate wood streete and the site/ground of 1 wich house of 6 leads in Pepper streete in WICHE aforesaid, all which premises are now in the tenure of the sd. Richard Wilbraham; for lives of the sd. Rauffe Wilbraham, Roger Wilbraham his son, and Thomas Wilbraham, son of Richard Wilbraham, son and heir of the sd. Richard Wilbraham, at an annual rent of £8, 40 strike of well made white salt of Shrewsburie measure heaped, or 20d. per strike in lieu thereof, and 6 Namptwiche cheeses to be made within Wiche Malbanke aforesaid, every cheese to contain 16lbs. weight.; to hold for the residue of the term and at the rents etc: therein specified, 12 September 1626 (CALS Ref: DWN/2/131).

**101.** See 89 and 90 above.

**102.** See 93 above.

**103.** See 97 above.

**104.** Lease by William Pearetree, clerk, executor of John Thrush, late of Wich Malbanke, Gentleman, to John Farrar, Shomaker, a pasture/croft called St Anns Croft or little frog Greaves, for a term of 3 lives, 4 April 1654 (CALS Ref: DWN/1/83).

**105.** Lease for 69 years, by Richard Wilberham of the Wiche Malbanke to Thomas Clutton of the sd. Wiche --- the tithe corn, hay, hemp, flax, wood and kidds of the township and fields of LEIGHTON, late in the tenure of Roger Broke, and also all that his part of 1 pasture in the parish of ACTON called Seint Anne croft or hospitall croft and all his part of the tithe corn of the township and fields of NEWBOLD, at an annual rent of 40/-. Cons. £22-6-8, 1 June 1555 (CALS Ref: DWN/2/85). & Assignment of Lease by Thomas Clutton of the Wiche Walbanke to Richard Wilberham the younger son of Richard Wilberham of the Wiche --- the tithe corn, hay, hemp, flax, wood and kids of the township and fields of LEIGHTON and also all his part of 1 pasture in the parish of ACTON called Seint Anne croft or hospitall croft and all his part of the tithe corn of the township and fields of NEWBOLD; to hold for the residue of a term of 69 years created by lease of 1. June 1555 from the sd. Richard Wilberham of the Wiche to the sd. Thomas Clutton, at an annual rent of 40/-; on condition that the sd. Richard Wilberham the younger will permit the sd. Richard Wilberham the elder and Elizabeth his wife and their assigns, for their lives and the life of the longer liver, to occupy and enjoy the sd. premises and the rents, issues and profits thereof, 3 June 1555 (CALS Ref: DWN/1/40).

**106.** Agreement between: William Pearetree, clerk, executor of John Thrush, late of Wich Malbanke, gentleman, deceased, and John Farrar of Wich Malbanke, shoemaker, one of the younger sons of John Farrar, gentleman, deceased, late son in law to the sd. John Thrush; and Roger Wilbraham of Wich Malbanke Esq.; reciting that WHEREAS the sd.

William Pearetree has by Indenture of 4. Apr. 1654 assigned to the sd. John Farrar the son, one croft with appurtenances called St. Anns croft, late in the holding of the sd. John Thrush, for the residue of a term determinable on the decease of Roger Wilbraham of Darfould Esq., and WHEREAS there is now in arrear to Roger Wilbraham, party to these presents, the sum of £55-12-8 for rent out of the sd. croft and other premises heretofore belonging to the Hospitall of St. Nicholas in WICH MALBANKE, the reversion whereof now belongs to the sd. Roger Wilbraham and his heirs, NOW the sd. William Pearetree and John Farrar, in consideration of the sd. £55-12-8 are agreed that the sd. Roger Wilbraham shall henceforward hold the sd. croft until such time as he shall out of the annual profits have received the sd. sum of £55-12-8, 7 April 1654 (CALS Ref: DWN/2/155).

**107.** Lease of a parcel of lands and possessions late of Richard Wrighte, in the county of Chester, in Monkes Copenhall, the tithes of Alvaston, in Hemhull, the chappell feld in WicheMalbanke and Acton, the chappell crofte and one salt house of six leaden fats, and the tithes belonging to the late chapel of St. Lawrence, by Queen Elizabeth, to John Brene, uncle to Margarett and Elizabeth Wrighte, the daughters and heirs of Richard Wrighte, gentleman, deceased, 6 June 1590 (CALS Ref: DWN/2/105).

**108.** Assignment of Lease by Thomas Clutton of the Wiche Walbanke to Richard Wilberham the younger son of Richard Wilberham of the Wiche --- the tithe corn, hay, hemp, flax, wood and kids of the township and fields of LEIGHTON and also all his part of 1 pasture in the parish of ACTON called Seint Anne croft or hospitall croft and all his part of the tithe corn of the township and fields of NEWBOLD; to hold for the residue of a term of 69 years created by lease of 1. June 1555 from the sd. Richard Wilberham of the Wiche to the sd. Thomas Clutton, at an annual rent of 40/-; on condition that the sd. Richard Wilberham the younger will permit the sd. Richard Wilberham the elder and Elizabeth his wife and their assigns, for their lives and the life of the longer liver, to occupy and enjoy the sd. premises and the rents, issues and profits thereof, 3 June 1555 (CALS Ref: DWN/1/40).

**109.** Lease for 69 years, by Richard Wilberham of the Wiche Malbanke to Thomas Clutton of the sd. Wiche --- the tithe corn, hay, hemp, flax, wood and kidds of the township and fields of LEIGHTON, late in the tenure of Roger Broke, and also all that his part of 1 pasture in the parish of ACTON called Seint Anne croft or hospitall croft and all his part of the tithe corn of the township and fields of NEWBOLD, at an annual rent of 40/-. Cons. £22-6-8, 1 June 1555 (CALS Ref: DWN/2/85).

**110.** Richard Leech son of Radulf Leech details his holdings by the gift and grant of his father, nominating his uncle John Leech heir thereto should he leave no issue. I Richard Leech, have the gift and grant of the aforesaid Radulf, one field or pasture called Frogge Polo in Wich Malbank, lying between land of William Davenport on one side and land of the Chapel of St. Laurence and land lately that of Richard Larketon on the other side for the term of 101 years, as more fully appears by indented charters. 23 November 1522. (Chetwode Papers, Keele University Ref: CH 194).

**111.** Lease by John Cheswis, of Mickley, Gentleman, to Richard Hewster, of Wyche Malbanke [Nantwich], Shoemaker, a croft in Henhull, lying between the lands of Thomas Chetwood and Thomas Aston on the East, and lands of the heirs of Richard Wright on the West, and the lands of Lawrence Wright on the North, and of the said Thomas Sparke on the South, 11$^{th}$ June 1590 (CALS Ref: DWN/2/106).

**112.** See 95 above.

**113.** Nantwich: Saxon to Puritan, Eric Garton, 1972, Page 77, and Footnote 5. Grant P.R.O. E318 8/11.

**114.** Gasquet lists three hospitals not mentioned so far, these being at Chester [1910, 266], Tarvin [op. cit., 308] and Wybunbury [op. cit., 317. ... The hospital mentioned by Gasquet at Wybunbury, occurring in 1464 and dedicated to St George and the Holy Cross, may be identical with a fraternity of the Holy Cross said to have existed at nearby Nantwich [Kettle, 1980, 126].

**115.** Trust: A History, Geoffrey Hosking, 2014, Page 74.

**116.** Nantwich: Saxon to Puritan, Eric Garton, 1972, Pages 88-89.

**117.** Feoffment by Hugh Jones, Citizen and Mercer of London, sells to Richard Wilbraham of Wich Malbanke, Gentleman, and Richard Wrighte of the same, Yeoman, his property in Namptwich near the church there, called the Guildhall, formerly belonging to the Guild or Fraternity, late in the tenure of the churchwardens, to hold of the Queen in free socage, for the consideration of £10, 26 May 1579 (CALS Ref: DWN/1/53).

**118.** The Trade Guilds and Fraternities, Johnsons' Nantwich Almanack and Directory, 1954, Page 111.

**119.** Notitia Cestriensis or Historical Notices of the Diocese of Chester, Rev. Francis Gastrell, Bishop of Chester (c1720), with notes by Rev. F. R. Raines, Volume I: Cheshire, The Chetham Society, First Series, Volume 8, 1845, Page 225, Footnote 9.

**120.** Confirmation by the Dean and Chapter of Lichifield, on behalf of Roger Bishop of Coventry and Lichfield, of which churches and chapels Combermere Abbey holds in Cheshire and Staffordshire, 9 May 1277 (CALS Ref: D5589/1).

**121.** Confirmation by Reginald, Bishop of Coventry and Lichfield, that after due examination of title, the Abbey holds the churches of Sandon and Alstonefield, Staffordshire and Little Ercall, Shropshire, 20 December 1456 (CALS Ref: D5589/4).

**122.** Appointment by Roger Plymmowth, Abbot of the House and Church of our Lady St Mary of Combermere, and the convent of the same, that Randulph of Wylbram as their procurator [their minister in charge of financial affairs], of the Chapel of our Lady St Mary of Nantwiche called the Nantwiche Chirche, for them to collect all the tithes, oblations, obventions, etc., belonging to the said Chapel and to render an account of the same, for 12 years, for which Randulph of Wylbram, is to receive an annual rent of 26 shillings and 8 pence issuing from their lands and tenements in Wyche Malbank [Nantwich], 4 September 1460 (CALS Ref: DWN/1/21).

**123.** Acton (Near Nantwich): The History of a Cheshire Parish and its seventeen townships, Edited by Frank A. Latham, 1995, Page 65.

# Acknowledgements

- **The Revd. Dr. Mark Hart**
  *(Rector of St Mary's Church, Nantwich)*
  *(Thank you for writing the Foreword for this book)*

- **Nantwich Museum**
  *(www.nantwichmuseum.org.uk)*

- **Janette Allotey**
  *(Nantwich Museum Research Group)*

- **Keith Harper**
  *(Nantwich Museum Research Group)*
  *(Thank you for creating the two maps after the Introduction for this book)*

- **Linda Briggs**
  *(Nantwich Museum Research Group)*
  *(Thank you for helping to transcribe and translate the c1380-1390 Rental of Knights Hospitaller properties in Nantwich deed)*

- **Andrew Lamberton, Keith Lawrence and Bernie Strawson**
  *(Nantwich Museum Research Group)*

- **Alistair Herbert-Jackson**
  *(Nantwich Resident)*

- **Dr Jessica Barker, FSA**
  *(Senior Lecturer in Medieval Art, The Courtauld Gallery)*
  **(for permission to use her photograph of 'Edward the Black Prince's Effigy's Sword Belt or Girdle, at Canterbury Cathedral' which appeared in "Fully armed in plate of war': making the effigy of the Black Prince, Jessica Barker, Graeme McArthur and Emily Pegues, The Burlington Magazine, Issue 163, November 2021, Pages 997-1009.')**

- **Canterbury Historical and Archaeological Society**
  *(https://www.canterbury-archaeology.org.uk/)*
  **(for permission to use two photographs of Henry Yevele)**

- **Caroline Picco**
  *(Cheshire Archives & Local Studies)*
  *(Thank you for helping to transcribe and translate the c1380-1390 Rental of Knights Hospitaller properties in Nantwich deed)*

- **Cheshire Archives & Local Studies**
  *(CALS was CRO (Cheshire Record Office))*

# Bibliography

*Books, Booklets, Journals:*

- Holinshed's Chronicles of England, Scotland, and Ireland, 1577. (http://www.cems.ox.ac.uk/holinshed/)

- The Vale Royal of England, Daniel King, 1656.

- Notitia Monastica, Thomas Tanner, 1744.

- An Historical Account of the Town and Parish of Nantwich, Joseph Partridge, 1774.

- The History of Cheshire: containing King's Vale-Royal Entire, Volume II, 1778.

- Magna Britannia: being A Concise Topographical Account of the Several Counties of Great Britain, Volume 2: Cambridgeshire, and the County Palatine of Chester, Rev. Daniel Lysons and Samuel Lysons, 1810.

- The History and Antiquities of Nantwich, in the County Palatine of Chester, J. W. Platt, 1818.

- Monasticon Anglicanum: A History of the Abbies and Other Monasteries, Hospitals, Frieries, and Cathedral and Collegiate Churches, with Their Dependencies, in England and Wales ... Originally Published in Latin, Volume 8, William Dugdale, 1825.

- Notitia Cestriensis or Historical Notices of the Diocese of Chester, Rev. Francis Gastrell, Bishop of Chester (c1720), with notes by Rev. F. R. Raines, Volume I: Cheshire, The Chetham Society, First Series, Volume 8, 1845.

- A Topographical Dictionary of England by Samuel Lewis 1848.

- Report on the Present State, and of the Proposed Restoration of the Parish Church of Nantwich, George Gilbert Scott, 1854.

- Inventories of Church Goods and Chantries in Cheshire, Temp Edward VI., The Historic Society of Lancashire and Cheshire, Volume 23 (1870-1872), Rev. Mackenzie E. C. Walcott, 27 January 1870, Pages 173-180.

- An Enquiry concerning Nantwich Church & Antiquities, Dates etc., Nantwich, Rev F G Blackburne, 6 Jun 1880. (CALS Ref: P 120/4525/131&133).

- The History of the County Palatine and City of Chester, Volume 1, 2, & 3, George Ormerod, 2nd Edition, Routledge, 1882.

- The Visitation of Cheshire, 1580, John Paul Rylands, 1882.

- A History of the Town and Parish of Nantwich or Wych-Malbank, Cheshire, James Hall, 1883 (Republished 1972).

- Annales Cestrienses Chronicle of the Abbey of St Werburg, at Chester, Edited by Richard Copley Christie, Record Society of Lancashire and Cheshire, 1887.

- The Book of the Abbot of Combermere: 1289 to 1529, Edited by James Hall, The Record Society of Lancashire and Cheshire, Volume 31, 1896.

- A Short History of Nantwich and Neighbourhood, Miss E. A. Johnson, revised and completed by Roger Russel, Johnson's Directory, Nantwich, 1902.

- W. Wonnacott, "Henry Yevely," Ars Quattuor Coronatorum, XXI, 1908.

- The Medieval Hospitals of England, Rotha Mary Clay, 1909.

- The Ledger Book of the Vale Royal Abbey, edited by John Brownbill, Manchester Record Society, 1914.

- The Hospital of St. Mary of Ospringe commonly called Maison Dieu, Charles H. Drake, Archaeologia Cantiana: Transactions of The Kent Archaeological Society, Volume 30, 1914.

- Betley Parish Registers [1538-1812], Edited by Percy W. L. Adams, 1916.

- Kelly's Directory of Cheshire, 1928.

- Fourteenth Century Steeple Building, Fred H. Crossley, Journal of Chester Archaeological Society, Volume 35, Part II, 1942.

- Henry Yevele, The Life of an English Architect, John Harvey, Journal of the Royal Society of Arts, Volume 93, Number 4696, (20 July 1945).

- Chronological Data Relating to the Churches of Cheshire, Fred H. Crossley, Transactions of the Lancashire and Cheshire Antiquarian Society, Volume LVII, 1943-1944, 1946.

- Henry Yevele: The Life of an English Architect, John H. Harvey, 1946.

- Old Cheshire Churches, Raymond Richards, 1947.

- The 600th Anniversary of Nantwich Parish Church, 1350-1950 Souvenir Programme, 1950.

- English Medieval Architects: A Biographical Dictionary down to 1550, 1954.

- Nantwich Almshouses and Charities, Johnsons Directory 1954, Pages 109-119.

- A Guide to The Church of S. Mary's, Nantwich, Cheshire, by Percy Newton Corry, May 1962.

- Cheshire Under the Three Edwards. A History of Cheshire, Volume 5, H. J. Hewitt, 1967.

- The Black Prince, H. J. Hewitt, Pages 322-328, Cheshire Round, Volume 1, No. 10, Summer 1969.

- The Place-names of Cheshire, J McN Dodgson, English Place-name Society, Volume XLVI, Part Three, The Place-names of Nantwich Hundred and Eddisbury Hundred, 1971.

- Nantwich, Saxon to Puritan: A History of the Hundred of Nantwich, C1050 to C1642, Eric Garton, 1972.

- The Quire and Misericords of St Mary's Parish Church, Nantwich, Cheshire, by Percy Newton Corry, 1974.

- In the Lifetime of Sir David Cradok, Kt, c1342-1390, Eric Garton, January 1976.

- Royal Administration of Cheshire Abbeys in the Late Middle Ages, Ann J Kettle, Cheshire History, Volume 4, 1979 Autumn, Pages 43 – 54.

- A History of the County of Chester: Volume 3. Originally published by Victoria County History, Various Authors, London, 1980.

- A History & Guide to Nantwich, J. J. Lake, 1982.

- A Templar Colony in North Staffordshire: Keele before the Sneyds, Dr Robin Studd, North Staffordshire Journal of Field Studies, Volume 22, 1982/5, Pages 5-21.

- The Great Fire of Nantwich, Jeremy Lake, 1983.

- The Buildings of England: Cheshire: Nikolaus Pevsner and Edward Hubbard, 1986.

- Master Masons of the Diocese of Lichfield: A Study in $14^{th}$-Century Architecture at the Time of the Black Death, J. M. Maddison, Transactions of the Lancashire and Cheshire Antiquarian Society, Volume 85, 1988.

- St Mary's, Nantwich: A Pitkin Guide, R. E. Pritchard, 1991.

- Cheshire Past: An Annual Review of Archaeology in Cheshire, Issue 4, Cheshire County Council, 1995.

- Acton (Near Nantwich): The History of a Cheshire Parish and its seventeen townships, Edited by Frank A. Latham, 1995.

- Buildings in Nantwich, Allan Whatley, Spring 1995.

- Monastic and Collegiate Cheshire, Roland W. Morant, 1996.

- The Church of Saint Mary, Nantwich: A history to the Dissolution of the Monasteries, 1536, Francis Blacklay, 1998.

- Historic Guide to Nantwich, Derek John Brownsword-Hulland, 1998.

- Wrenbury and Marbury, Local History Group, F. A. Latham (editor), 1999.

- The Military Personnel of Edward the Black Prince, David S. Green, Medieval Prosopography, Volume 21, 2000.

- Edward, Prince of Wales and Aquitaine: A Biography of the Black Prince, Richard Barber, 2002.

- Cheshire Historic Towns Survey: Wybunbury Archaeological Assessment, Cheshire County Council, Mike Shaw & Jo Clark, 2003.

- Lost Houses in Nantwich, Andrew Lamberton & Robin Gray, 2005.

- A Templar Chapel at Onneley, Michael Fradley, Journal of the Staffordshire Archaeological Society, Volume XLII, 2008.

- Misericords of North West England: Their Nature and Significance, John Dickinson, 2008.

- Early Nantwich Deeds, Allan Murray Wilson, 2010.

- Acton: Through the Ages, Gerald Emerton, 2010.

- Cheshire and the Crusades, Kathryn Hurlock, 2011; Transactions of the Historic Society of Lancashire and Cheshire, Vol. 159.

- Guilds and Related Organisations in Great Britain and Ireland: A Bibliography, compiled by Tom Hoffman, 2011.

- Crutched Friars and Crosiers: The Canons Regular of the Order of the Holy Cross in England and France, J. Michael Hayden, 2013.

- Trust: A History, Geoffrey Hosking, 2014.

- The Knights Templar Chapel, Onneley, North Staffordshire, Charles E. S. Fairey, December 2013 (Revised 2015). (https://sites.google.com/site/charlesfaireyhistorian/publications/knights-templar-chapel-onneley)

- Interpreting Medieval Corbel Sculpture, Richard Halsey, Historic Churches, 2015. (https://www.buildingconservation.com/articles/medieval-corbel-sculpture/medieval-corbel-sculpture.htm)

- The Devils of Audley, Barthomley and Betley, Charles E. S. Fairey, September 2016 (Revised 2017). (https://sites.google.com/site/charlesfaireyhistorian/publications/the-devils-of-audley-barthomley-and-betley)

- Chester Cathedral Guidebook, Jessica Hodge, 2017.

- Keele's Templar Window and the Templars Jacques de Molay & Thomas Totty, Dr Robin Studd, 2018.

- Lost Buildings of Welsh Row, Nantwich, Andrew Lamberton, Nantwich Museum Booklet, 2018.

- Church Orientation, Alignment and Solar Worship; with Examples from Cheshire and North Staffordshire, Charles E. S. Fairey, 2018. (https://www.mysticmasque.com/history-mystery/church-orientation-alignment-and-solar-worship)

- Nantwich Pubs, Andrew Lamberton and Bill Pearson, 2018.

- The Lost Chapel and the Pubs of Barthomley, Charles E. S. Fairey, 2019 (Rev 2020). (https://sites.google.com/site/charlesfaireyhistorian/publications/the-lost-chapel-and-the-pubs-of-barthomley)

- Nantwich Tanneries, Andrew Lamberton and Glynn Skerratt, 2020.

- 'Fully armed in plate of war': making the effigy of the Black Prince, Jessica Barker, Graeme McArthur and Emily Pegues, The Burlington Magazine, Issue 163, November 2021, Pages 997-1009.

- The History of Weston (South Cheshire), $2^{nd}$ Edition, Charles E. S. Fairey, 2023- (unpublished $2^{nd}$ Edition).

- The Cheshire Sheaf.

- The Chetham Society.

- Journals of the Historic Society of Lancashire & Cheshire.

- Journals of the Record Society of Lancashire and Cheshire.

- Transactions of the Lancashire and Cheshire Antiquarian Society.

*Maps:*

- Map of Nantwich by Joseph Fenna, 1794.

- Board of Health Map of Nantwich, 1851, Scale 1:528 (ten-foot to the mile).

- Ordnance Survey Town Plan of Nantwich, 1876, Scale 1:528 (ten-foot to the mile).

- Cheshire Tithe Maps (https://maps.cheshireeast.gov.uk/tithemaps/)

*Video / Television:*

- The Crusades (Documentary), TV Mini Series, 2012.

- The Black Prince – England's Warrior Prince Documentary, YouTube Channel: The People Profiles, 7 Aug 2020. (https://www.youtube.com/watch?v=FKgekOeftr4)

- Edward III – England's Greatest King Documentary, YouTube Channel: The People Profiles, 31 Dec 2021. (https://www.youtube.com/watch?v=p3lb1pKYl08)

- Various, YouTube Channel: Real Crusades History. (https://www.youtube.com/channel/UCpiumHmUE5EZeLTftxv9qGw)

- Military Effigies of the Yorkist Age, Mark Downing, YouTube Channel: The Churches Conservation Trust, 24 August 2021. (https://www.youtube.com/watch?v=y9Kr_Y_mzfY)

- The Leper Hospital, Winchester, Hampshire, Time Team, Season 8: Episode 13, Aired 1st April 2001.

- Governor's Green (St Nicholas' Hospital), Portsmouth, Time Team, Season 17: Episode 10, Aired 24th October 2010.

*Websites:*

- **Charles E. S. Fairey, Historian** (https://sites.google.com/site/charlesfaireyhistorian/)

- **National Archives Catalogue via Discovery** (https://discovery.nationalarchives.gov.uk)

- **Cheshire Archives & Local Studies Catalogue** (http://catalogue.cheshirearchives.org.uk/calmview/)

- **Find My Past** (https://www.findmypast.co.uk/)

- **Heritage Gateway (was Pastscape)** (https://www.heritagegateway.org.uk/gateway/)

- **British Listed Buildings** (https://britishlistedbuildings.co.uk/)

- **The British Newspaper Archive** (https://www.britishnewspaperarchive.co.uk/)

- **Tracing the Past: Medieval Vaults: Nantwich:** (https://www.tracingthepast.org.uk/2021/04/08/nantwich_site_by_site/, and https://www.tracingthepast.org.uk/2021/04/08/nantwich_history/)

- **A Dabber's Nantwich Website: Cottage may be on the site of a 13th century priory or hospital, Andrew Lamberton:** (http://www.dabbersnantwich.me.uk/oldpix23.htm)

- **History of Combermere Abbey:** (http://www.combermere-restoration.co.uk/the-wicked-monks-of-combermere/)

Printed in Great Britain
by Amazon